Advance praise for
The History of Loyola Basketball

"Only a seasoned journalist like Fred Mitchell could uncover the fascinating stories behind the Ramblers' glorious journey to the NCAA championship. Mitchell details surprising, 'behind-the-curtain' events, which carry the reader on a breathtaking trip to an unexpected, hard-fought victory."

—ROBERT JORDAN, JR., Ph.D., Loyola University,
Retired Anchor/Reporter, WGN TV Chicago

THE HISTORY OF
LOYOLA BASKETBALL
MORE THAN A SHOT AND A PRAYER

FRED MITCHELL

Post Hill
PRESS

A POST HILL PRESS BOOK

The History of Loyola Basketball:
More Than a Shot and a Prayer
© 2019 by Fred Mitchell
All Rights Reserved

ISBN: 978-1-64293-065-8
ISBN (eBook): 978-1-64293-066-5

Cover art by Cody Corcoran
Cover photo by Karen Callaway of Chicago Catholic News Service
Interior design and composition by Greg Johnson, Textbook Perfect

Post Hill Press
New York • Nashville
posthillpress.com
Published in the United States of America

Contents

Preface

Growing up a Chicago sports fan and later becoming a Chicago sportswriter afforded me an unobstructed view of the city's college and professional teams as they succeeded and failed.

For four decades I accrued enough media credentials to decorate a Christmas tree. I was the only sportswriter in Chicago Tribune history to be the main beat reporter covering the Cubs, Bears and Bulls as a main assignment. But that was just for starters.

I also covered Loyola basketball, DePaul, Northwestern, Northern Illinois, Illinois-Chicago, the WNBA, the White Sox, Arena Football, high school sports, the Olympics, the World Series, NBA Finals, Super Bowls, NCAA basketball tournaments, college bowl games and surely a few others that I have forgotten. I also wrote the "Around Town" column for more than a decade as I weighed in on fascinating topics intersecting sports, society, media and entertainment.

The names and faces of coaches and players come and go in all of sports over the years, but the drama and the impact they make can be everlasting. And so it was for the Loyola Ramblers, both old and new. I am old enough to remember vividly the exhilaration created when the 1963 Ramblers team shocked the sports world by upending two-time defending national champion Cincinnati in the NCAA championship game held in Louisville, Kentucky.

The ramifications from coach George Ireland's bold decision to start four African-American players during a period of such racial tension, particularly in the South, created a stir that ultimately impacted the entire game of basketball. In later years, when I became a sportswriter, I got to know Ireland personally and realized the genuine sincerity of his mission.

There are so many layers to the history of Chicago sports, and I was fortunate enough to span more than four decades with the newspaper to witness many events up close and meet so many of the fascinating headliners. Whether it was George Halas, Jesse Owens, Gale Sayers, Muhammad Ali, Ernie Banks, Walter Payton, Dick Butkus, Bobby Hull, Stan Mikita, Isiah Thomas, Ray Meyer, Mark Aguirre, Michael Jordan...I could name-drop forever.

In the end, it will be the people and the events they created that I will most remember. And what the Loyola basketball team was able to accomplish in the 2017–18 season—making it to the Final Four for the first time since 1963—ranks right up there with any of the previous stories I have been able to follow and chronicle.

With the Cubs winning the World Series in 2016, the White Sox winning the World Series in 2005, Northwestern being invited to the NCAA men's basketball tournament for the first time in school history in 2017...the Ramblers' improbable run with Sister Jean by their side perhaps was most stunning and surprising to me. And who doesn't love a pleasant surprise when it comes to the sometimes grudgingly predictable world of sports?

This is my 12th sports book and I would like to say that I have seen it all when it comes to improbable sports stories. But I am certain I have not. And that's what makes the world of sports so unpredictable and fascinating. I hope you will enjoy the ride and the stories that follow.

—Fred Mitchell

Introduction

Everyone loves a feel-good story, one that is not embellished, rehearsed or perhaps even widely anticipated.

Surprise! Here come the 2017–18 Loyola Ramblers from relative national college basketball obscurity, advancing to the Final Four and leading powerhouse Michigan in the second half of the NCAA Tournament semifinal game before finally succumbing to the favored Wolverines.

Here comes a vastly underrated Loyola team with 99-year-old Sister Jean accompanying the squad, rendering pregame prayers and offering timely advice and encouragement. She unwittingly becomes the center of attention, holding her own news conferences on a national stage while a bobblehead of her likeness breaks sales records and social media videos of her go viral.

Here comes Loyola with a pragmatic, genuine, unassuming head coach, Porter Moser, known for doing things the right way and encouraging his players to "buy in to the culture of the program" that stresses building character, playing with good sportsmanship and teamwork and respecting the process. What a refreshing story line during a college basketball season overloaded with headlines about recruiting violations and other scandals.

Much of the nation fell in love with Sister Jean and admired the grit and determination of Loyola's relatively unheralded players.

The fabric of this team is woven into the initial threads of the 1963 NCAA championship Loyola squad that not only captured a national title but also made historical strides for college basketball and the nation with regard to civil rights and racial integration.

This story must be properly told through the voices of those who actually took part in the joyful games as well as the painful incidents that represent a significant part of our country's history.

The Makings of a Winner

Porter Moser rolled up a sleeve on his snug-fitting shirt, fully exposing his muscular left bicep.

"See! I am still getting chills just talking about what we did three months ago," the energetic Loyola basketball coach said with a broad smile, perched comfortably in his office chair.

"They are sincere chills."

His Loyola Ramblers gave college basketball fans in Chicago and around the world sincere chills by astoundingly advancing to the 2018 NCAA Final Four.

The school's historic 1963 NCAA championship team had provided the original template for student-athlete success on and off the court for the well-respected Chicago-area institution along the shores of Lake Michigan in the Rogers Park neighborhood. But that latest run seemingly came out of nowhere before winding up on everyone's radar, television screen and mobile device.

Moser began assembling the ingredients for a winning program as soon as he arrived on the Loyola campus some eight years ago, taking over for Jim Whitesell, who had compiled a 109–107 record from 2004 through 2011 while coaching his team in the Horizon League. Moser recruited players from winning high school programs who had the proper character, selflessness, work ethic and basketball skills to make the Ramblers winners.

It certainly did not happen overnight, as much as Moser and Loyola fans would have liked it to occur. His Loyola team was 1–17 in the conference and 7–23 overall his first season. But he constantly preached that it would be a dedicated process, and at long last his diligence is paying off.

Moser has not taken any shortcuts to establish a winning culture around his program, and he has put his prophetic words into action. His players have displayed maturity, poise and humility, not to mention court discipline, patience and determination to win.

The Ramblers captured the 2018 Missouri Valley regular-season title and MVC tournament championship to earn the automatic NCAA Tournament bid. Then Loyola promptly dispatched Miami (64–62), Tennessee (63–62), Nevada (69–68), and Kansas State (78–62) before losing to third-seeded Michigan (69–57) in the Final Four semifinal contest in San Antonio, Texas. The Ramblers finished with a school-record 32 wins and a 32–6 record.

Loyola even received the support from the 44th president of the United States, Barack Obama, a zealous basketball fan and a proud Chicagoan. Prior to the game against Michigan, Obama tweeted, "Incredible to have a Chicago team in the Final Four. I'll take that over an intact bracket any day! Good luck to all @LoyolaChicago. Let's keep it going!"

The unexpected success during the 2017–18 season did not go unnoticed by Chicago sports fans hungry for positive news. And Moser and his players became the toast of the entire state of Illinois, making appearances as special guests of the Chicago Blackhawks, Cubs, Bulls and White Sox. A trip downstate to Springfield for special recognition in front of lawmakers was also on the schedule.

Life for Porter Moser would never be the same.

"Take my normal routine and just throw it out the window," Moser said months after the 2017–18 season. "Every day I walk in, my secretary, Megan, looks at me and has 10 new things. But it is a good busy. I am not wired not to be active. I have a hard time saying no because I am being asked so many things. But I think the coolest part of this journey is that I grew up a die-hard Chicago sports fan. The Cubs, Bears, the Bulls, the Blackhawks...I was the guy....I went to Ray Meyer's basketball camp in Wisconsin. That wasn't like a two-night day camp. It was overnight for two weeks. And those DePaul teams then were a huge part of the Chicago sports scene."

Meyer's prolific DePaul teams of the late '70s and early '80s captured more attention locally than the Chicago Bulls of the NBA. Those Blue Demon squads led by future NBA stars Mark Aguirre and Terry Cummings gave a young Moser a glimpse of what it looks like to be adored by the sports fans of Chicago.

Meyer coached DePaul to 21 postseason appearances. He coached teams that twice made it to the Final Four (1943 and 1979), and in 1945 won the NIT. The rivalry with Loyola was at its height during Meyer's coaching tenure at DePaul, from 1942 to 1984. His overall head coaching record was 724–354.

Meyer once told me that college basketball coaches in this era are under much greater scrutiny than he was in the midst of his career. DePaul endured several lean years under his tutelage, but the school administration stuck with him. He repaid their patience with championship-caliber squads later on.

"The pressure to win is so great. When I was coaching, you could schedule any school you wanted to play," Meyer told me in 2003, three years before he died at 92. "You didn't have to worry about how much money you were going to make. I know a couple of coaches—I don't want to mention their names—who were told before the season started that if they didn't make the NCAA Tournament, they would be gone. It's not fair. It's all about money."

Among his accomplishments, way back in the early 1940s, Meyer was credited with molding center George Mikan into an All-American and future NBA star.

Along the way, basketball fans in the Midwest took notice, including Moser when he was a youngster.

"And to know that we have a piece of history in Chicago sports...that has meant so much to me," Moser says now of his Loyola achievers. "And one of the coolest things that has happened has been the complete embrace by the city of Chicago."

Following his team's magnificent Final Four run, Moser became a frequent television and radio guest in the press box at Wrigley Field during Cubs broadcasts, basking in the glow of Loyola's success. Living the dream.

"Everywhere I have been and everywhere our players go... sometimes after a game people come up to you and say, 'Nice game, nice job.' And the overwhelming response...almost to 100 percent...is just, 'Thank you. Thank you for doing this for Chicago. Thank you for doing it the right way. Thank you for going on this run. You connected our alumni group. You connected Chicago,'" he said.

"That has meant so much to me. This embrace. That is what I didn't get when we were in the middle of it. Because I was just focused on winning the next game. And then the weeks after that, being out and about, it has been just overwhelming how much this has meant to Chicago. And then to have the nation looking at us and saying, 'Hey, you did it with great kids, great student-athletes who played together and played hard.'"

Moser has been rightfully recognized for his accomplishments. He was named Missouri Valley Coach of the Year and he was picked National Association of Basketball Coaches (NABC) District 16 Coach of the Year.

The last Loyola coach to earn conference Coach of the Year was Gene Sullivan in 1985, when the Ramblers were in the Midwestern Collegiate Conference. Moser became one of only five people to have won the MVC regular-season title as both a player (at Creighton) and a coach.

Moser often defers credit to his assistant coaches, including associate head coach Bryan Mullins and assistants Drew Valentine and Matt Gordon. The director of basketball operations is Jevon Mamon, and the video coordinator is London Dokubo.

"When we first took over this job, everyone told us it was going to be hard because this is a pro town," Moser said. "But I always said to myself to keep me fired up, 'This is a *sports* town.' They love and respect a good sports story and get behind it. And I am hoping that continues. Because to see that arena get filled at the end of the year for the Illinois State game...it really makes a difference."

The Illinois State game drew a capacity 4,963 fans into the cozy Gentile Arena.

"We are going to have a target on our backs. Every arena that we go into is going to be full," Moser said. "We've got to create that home-court atmosphere here and I think it is going to happen."

Loyola, a university with a listed overall enrollment of 16,673, provided enough excitement during the 2017–18 regular season to encourage greater fan support. The Ramblers captured the program's first-ever road win against a top-five opponent when they beat then-fifth-ranked Florida 65–59 at Gainesville on Dec. 6. For the season, Loyola defeated four nationally ranked teams.

As a former guard at Creighton University and a longtime coach, Moser understands that there are life lessons to be learned through both victories and losses. After his Ramblers squandered a halftime lead to Michigan in the NCAA semifinal game, Moser quickly put the loss into perspective during his postgame news conference.

"Congrats to Michigan. They played a great game. They did what great teams do. They capitalized on that run where we made six turnovers in a row," Moser said. "I want to congratulate them, but I also stand here, sit here, and cannot be more proud of a group than I am of this group.

"And when I walked off the floor, I was asked what I said to them. And what I said to them was, 'The more you invest in something, the harder it is to give up.' And they didn't want to end it. And they have so much to be proud of. They changed the perception of a program. They changed the perception of when you say Loyola Chicago, for men's basketball. They changed that, the perception of it.

"They impacted so many lives…not only starting with our campus, and then it spread on. High-character kids playing their tails off unselfishly. I couldn't be more proud, and saddened, that this is over with these kids. And this group, high character and a fun group to be around, [more] than I've ever been around."

Moser also spoke about the life lessons learned through intense competition.

"Like I told these guys, I said, 'We're going to be connected for life,'" he said. "I tell them in the recruiting process, 'You're not making a four-year commitment at Loyola to play for us, you're making a lifetime relationship.' And that's what we have. That's what these guys have. It's a lifetime relationship. And it's not a four-year commitment. And I'm proud of that. I'm proud of that, that they used the word 'family' all the time. You hear that word all the time with this group. I love that. Means a lot to me."

An example of the family atmosphere on the 2017–18 Loyola team was the relationship between outgoing senior Ben Richardson and his high school teammate and lifelong friend Clayton Custer. The two had been teammates since the third grade in Overland Park, Kansas.

Richardson spoke about their relationship after the tournament semifinal loss to Michigan.

"It hurts to have this be the last one," Richardson said. "We wish that it could have ended better. We believe that we could have gone on. But I'm proud of myself. I'm proud of each and every one of these guys, and I'm proud of Clay."

Richardson had encouraged Custer to transfer from Iowa State to join him at Loyola, where the two combined for over eight assists a game.

"Nothing made me happier than taking the floor with him and compete with him. Having him join me in Chicago was a dream come true, and we did a lot of things that people probably didn't think that we could do," Richardson said. "And we proved a lot of people wrong. And I love that guy to death, and we'll never forget this."

Custer wound up winning the Larry Bird Missouri Valley Player of the Year award. And Richardson was the MVC Defensive Player of the Year. Cameron Krutwig, a 6–9 center, was named MVC Freshman of the Year.

Richardson also heaped praise on Moser for his overall coaching approach throughout the season.

"Yeah, there's a lot of things that I learned, life lessons, from this guy. And I couldn't be happier to have chosen Loyola and come to Chicago and played for him," Richardson told reporters after the loss to Michigan.

"And as far as preparing for Michigan, we prepare just like everybody else. He's super detail-oriented. And we were ready for everything that they were going to throw at us. Obviously, we didn't execute some of our game plan like we wanted to.

"But just the way that we've continuously been prepped for every team we face this year, and whether it's film, walk-throughs, you know, practices and then extra walk-throughs just in ballrooms, we'll set it up wherever we can just to get a competitive advantage.

"And that's something that he's always been really passionate about, giving us that confidence, because by the time the game comes, we have prepped so much that we have a real confidence we'll win the game because we know what they're going to throw at us. And I think the way that he's done that has really propelled us and helped us in this tournament. Obviously, tonight we didn't execute the game plan well enough."

Taking a mid-major school to the Final Four meant intense speculation that Moser would be courted by bigger schools and perhaps leave when his contract expired with Loyola. But he signed a lucrative contract extension.

"It worked out great," he said. "I wasn't going to talk to anybody until we got done playing. I was approached through many back channels and I just wouldn't talk to anybody. I said, 'How can I look at my players and tell them to have laser-like focus and to be all-in during our run?'

"People were antsy for jobs, and there was something where...it was something special for me to see the embrace of Chicago. I had a friend tell me, 'Don't run from happiness.' And you know what? I am happy. I love the people I work with, I love the guys on our team. And I didn't want to run from that for the money.

"And I am not saying I won't. So I don't want to be a hypocrite. But I am really happy right now. I just want to see us commit...like this (new) practice facility is huge. We can't continue without it. We've gone seven years without a place for these student-athletes to practice. It's going to be another year. But at least the ground is broken. I want to win and I believe we can do that consistently, and I love Chicago and I love the people I work with and my family loves it here and I am from this area."

Moser's competitive spirit is part of the reason he embraces the challenge of making Loyola a consistent conference and national contender while maintaining the academic integrity of the school.

"I am the youngest of four and I had two older brothers," he said. "And we were just a competitive family. We were playing board games, card games, and I was always trying to play with my older brothers and friends. I just wanted to compete so bad and play with them. I hate to lose. I couldn't stand to lose. I love the euphoria of winning.

"Whether it was euchre, whether it was Scrabble or Monopoly…I wanted to win. I learned at a young age that you can control what you can control. And I always felt I could control my work ethic and my attitude and my energy. Those three things. And I always tell my guys to dominate what they can control. And I learned that at a young age."

Moser started two years at Creighton and helped the Bluejays win the 1989 Missouri Valley Conference title as well as an NCAA Tournament berth.

In high school he excelled at Benet Academy in suburban Lisle, Illinois, where he started three years on the varsity squad. He was named conference player of the year as a senior. Benet Academy was 70–14 during Moser's three years on the varsity, playing for coach Bill Geist. Benet won three East Suburban Catholic Conference championships with Moser, who was a three-time all-conference player and two-time all-area selection.

In 2017 Moser was named to the Illinois Basketball Coaches Association Hall of Fame for his accomplishments as a player.

"I wasn't the most talented guy in college ball by any stretch of the imagination," Moser says modestly. "But what I could control was how hard I worked and all that. I think it kind of stems from trying to compete with my brothers."

Moser remains intent on having the full backing of Loyola's administration and alumni to accomplish his long-term mission with the school's basketball program.

"I hope this (success) attracts alumni, past and present, from different generations, to step up," Moser said. "Pride is an awesome thing. And I think the pride that was coming out across the country about Loyola was great.

"You look at some of these other programs like Gonzaga, Wichita State and Butler...they invested. They had fan bases invest in the future. We haven't had that. There hasn't been a huge investment to athletics. And I am hoping this sparks it. Look what it has done to this university. It has changed the way that you say 'Loyola.' Our admissions office, they said admissions at Loyola will never be the same. That is a powerful statement. So I hope people understand that this run impacted the school, so let's invest in it. Let's feed it. I am not saying to me personally. I am saying to this program, this practice facility, the things we can do for the athletes' well-being, so we are not just clawing to every dollar. Upgrade the infrastructure."

Major college basketball, no doubt, is big business. And the cycle for sustained success revolves around television revenue, home attendance, alumni support and general fan backing.

"In terms of the fan base, we still finished last in attendance last year," Moser noted. "It is the first time that a Missouri Valley champion has finished last in attendance. It has never happened before, ever. That can't be. We now have a target on our back and we really have to create a home-court atmosphere.

"As many people who jumped on our bandwagon, we have got to be able to draw 5,000 a night. We just have to. We have 6,000 students (living) on this campus. It makes a difference. I think everyone had fun on the journey and that has to snowball. It is hard for recruiting when a TV game comes on and there is a whole empty section in a 5,000-seat arena."

Thousands of previously uncommitted fans gleefully cheered for Loyola through its magical NCAA Tournament run of 2018.

"You can't put a number on the advertising and marketing value that Loyola-Chicago got worldwide." Moser said. "They are putting numbers on it and it sounds like it is exceeding a billion dollars, I heard. Isn't that crazy? Name another department that can have that kind of impact. I hope this ignites a commitment."

Donations to Loyola's athletic programs increased 660 percent from the year before the Ramblers' Final Four appearance, according to the *Chicago Business Journal*. The school received 31 percent more requests about the school than in the previous year. And Loyola's social media engagement skyrocketed 1,676 percent. Website traffic grew 91 percent and social media followers went up 34 percent.

Tom Soboro, Loyola's senior associate athletic director for external operations, told the publication that all of the extra revenue would be directed toward the athletic program, as opposed to branding and advertising ventures.

So many academic leaders at colleges throughout the country become leery when it comes to making a commitment to upgrade and sustain revenue-generating athletic programs. But one does not necessarily negate the other.

Loyola basketball players had a cumulative 3.1 grade-point average in the spring of 2018.

"We have the No. 1 graduation rate in the country. The last two years it has been Loyola and Harvard," Moser stated. "This is put out by the NCAA. Every one of our guys has graduated. Every year. So we 100 percent do not dismiss academics. So you can have both.

"A lot of schools think that if you invest in basketball, then you automatically are dismissing academics. We are hopefully proving that to anybody on this campus and anyone else that we are doing both. We are graduating our athletes and we are making it to the Final Four."

The goal of erecting a new practice facility could go a long way in terms of attracting strong recruits. The Alfie Norville Practice Facility could put Loyola on a par with peer institutions in the Missouri Valley. Al Norville, a 1960 Loyola alumnus and a member of the school's athletic hall of fame, donated the cornerstone gift of $1 million for the project.

The practice facility will be named in honor of Al's late wife, Alfena.

Norville, as a player at Loyola, averaged 13.7 points and 8.9 rebounds in 62 career games. He was a 70 percent free-throw shooter.

Loyola produced its first NBA player in 30 years when Milton Doyle played for the Brooklyn Nets during the 2017–18 season.

Doyle, a 6–4 guard, starred at Marshall High School in Chicago before accepting a scholarship to Kansas. He transferred to Loyola before the start of his freshman year at Kansas following a summer tour to Europe, and had to sit out a year before emerging as a pro prospect when he became the first Loyola player to be named to the MVC first team.

Doyle said the main reason he wanted to leave Kansas was because he was homesick and he wanted to make a major impact on an up-and-coming program. As a redshirt freshman, Doyle started all 32 games for the Ramblers and was named MVC Newcomer of the Year and Freshman of the Year. He became the first Rambler to lead the team in scoring (14.9), assists (3.6), steals (1.2) and blocks (0.7).

After a few brief stints with the Nets, Doyle signed a contract on Aug. 8, 2018, with UCAM Murcia of the Liga ACB in Spain.

Several other former Loyola players have had at least a taste of action in either the NBA or the ABA, including Andre Wakefield (1979–80), Wayne Sappleton (1985), Mickey Rottner (1947–48), Mike Novak (1949–50), Jerry Nagel (1950), Andre Moore (1988), LaRue Martin (1973–76), Jack Kerris (1950–53), Wilbert Kautz (1947), Les Hunter (1965–73), Alfredrick Hughes (1985), Jerry Harkness (1964–69), Don Hanrahan (1953), Ed Earle (1954) and Jack Dwan (1949).

Despite the Ramblers' success in the 2017–18 season and NCAA Tournament, prognosticators failed to rank Loyola among the best returning squads for 2018–19. Moser was neither fazed nor surprised.

"We've got to have guys step up. The guys who are returning have got to get better," he said. "Preseason predictions only matter within your own locker room. Like, it is only what we believe in. We talk about getting better and all that. People don't know how good Marques Townes, who sat out (the 2016–17 season after transferring into Loyola), is going to be.

"People don't know about Luol Deng's cousin (6–7 forward Aher Uguak), who was sitting out. We do because we are with him every day. People don't know how hard some of our guys are working. So we don't put much stock in it. I am obsessed with getting that culture, that connection. I am obsessed with getting each guy better. We are such a tight group that all of those little things matter.

"I don't want to be sitting here talking about winning another Missouri Valley championship or getting back to the Final Four. That's backwards thinking. I want to attack another championship. I want to attack our culture and get better at all of those things. Spending time on a person's prediction is a waste of time."

The average height on the 2017–18 Loyola team was just 6–4 and the average years of playing experience was 1.6. So how did this group manage to come within just one victory of competing for a national championship?

It had to have been unquantifiable unselfishness, determination, focus and discipline.

No Rambler averaged more than 13.2 points a game. Yet five players averaged double figures in scoring as Loyola made its first NCAA Tournament appearance in 33 years. The win over Illinois State on March 4, 2018, was Loyola's 10th in a row. The Ramblers would go on to win four more before falling to Michigan in the national semifinal game.

Rick Majerus, who died of heart failure at 64 in 2012, was an important mentor for Moser, who was an assistant coach at Saint Louis University before taking the head coaching position at Loyola in 2011. Moser says he still has Majerus' phone number in his directory and retains vivid memories of the former successful college coach.

Majerus had been a head coach at Ball State and Utah and took the Utes to the Final Four in 1998. During his four years as an assistant to Majerus at Saint Louis, Moser said he learned the importance of emphasizing the details with his players, whether it was spacing on offense, gritty determination on defense or learning to have fun playing the game along the way.

Moser's head coaching résumé includes a 54–34 record in three seasons at Arkansas-Little Rock. He was hired by Illinois State in 2003, where he was 51–67 before being fired with three years left on his contract. That's when Moser decided to join Majerus as an assistant coach with the Billikens so he could "learn from the genius."

Majerus was renowned for his insatiable appetite and late-night meals, as well as his dedicated work ethic. And yet the life-long bachelor impressed upon Moser to keep his family first on the list of life priorities.

Very tangibly, Moser has perpetuated Majerus' legacy with a "Wall of Culture" at Loyola in the middle of the Ramblers' locker room. Moser learned many of the fundamentals from working with Majerus for four years.

The Wall of Culture has fundamental sayings like "Reach for the Lights" when describing how to defend a shot. "Never quit on a play" or "Never be three in a row" when it comes to creating a passing lane between the ball and the defender.

Moser, the father of four, declares rightfully, "I was meant to be here."

Loyola's success in the 2017–18 season revived hope that the Chicago-area college basketball programs could indeed take center stage among the nation's elite.

Northwestern made it to the NCAA men's tournament for the first time in school history in 2017. But schools such as Illinois, Northern Illinois, UIC, DePaul and others have struggled to win on a regular basis.

It certainly is not that Chicago is bereft of super-talented high school players. Over the past decade alone, Chicago-area standouts like Derrick Rose, Jabari Parker, Jalen Brunson, Cliff Alexander, Anthony Turner and Jahlil Okafor have opted to play college basketball outside of the Chicago area. Not to mention the college decisions years further back of Chicagoans such as Isiah Thomas (Indiana), Dwyane Wade (Marquette), Glenn "Doc" Rivers (Marquette) and Maurice Cheeks (West Texas A&M).

Back in the '80s, Loyola was able snag Phillips High School guard Carl Golston, who was first-team all-conference in 1984 and '86.

DePaul achieved its success during Meyer's era when local stars such as Aguirre, Cummings and Dave Corzine decided to stay in Chicago for their college ball before moving on to the NBA.

Aguirre campaigned for the vacant head coaching job at DePaul in recent years, feeling he was most qualified to tap into the local talent and make the Blue Demons relevant again. But to no avail.

Loyola has managed to recruit players from the Chicago Public Schools system in recent years, and it has paid off with the likes of Milton Doyle from Marshall and Donte Ingram, who was a key player out of Chicago basketball powerhouse Simeon High School. Ingram was Loyola's first recruit from Simeon since Tim Bankston in 1986.

Finding sustained success at Loyola has been a daunting task for coaches past and present.

Larry Farmer (71–102), Ken Burmeister (40–71) and Will Rey (45–96) can attest to that. In fact, Moser, Sullivan (149–114), Ireland (321–255), Tom Haggerty (111–41) and Lenny Sachs (224–129) have been the only ones with significant stretches of winning teams in school history.

Sister Jean

Sister Jean Dolores-Schmidt sat comfortably behind her desk, smiling radiantly in her glass-enclosed office, situated within easy access of the Loyola University student center.

She recalled wistfully the highlights of a life well spent, identifying herself by name and affiliation, as if anyone paying attention to college basketball would not know her name, faith and enduring image.

"My name is Sister Jean Dolores-Schmidt. Everybody calls me Sister Jean. I am a sister from the very Blessed Virgin Mary. Our house is in Dubuque, Iowa," she recited dutifully.

Any fair and comprehensive account of the Loyola basketball program would not be complete without the proper acknowledgment of the charismatic 99-year-old Sister Jean and her positive impact on the program.

Sister Jean has been the team's beloved chaplain and inspirational leader since 1994. But her national and indeed international celebrity really took off during the 2018 NCAA basketball tournament as television cameras followed her entrance via wheelchair into arenas across the country and focused on her expressions and reactions courtside during the games. And broadcasters invariably commented on the spiritual and emotional impact she had on the Loyola players, coaches, university and ever-growing fan base.

Five thousand Sister Jean bobbleheads were sold in just 48 hours during the 2018 tournament, a record for the Bobblehead Hall of Fame. That was in addition to all the T-shirts and socks that bear her likeness. A total of 18,980 of her bobbleheads were manufactured by June of 2018 and distributed, with many more on the way.

During the Final Four in San Antonio, Sister Jean held court at her own designated news conference in a standing-room-only facility with media members who dropped their usual cynicism for an odd combination of reverence and levity.

"It looked like Tom Brady at the Super Bowl," Moser quipped at the time. Subsequently, Sister Jean was ranked No. 24 on *People* magazine's Top 100 list of reasons to love America.

"This is the most fun I've had in my life. It is," the smiling Sister Jean said earnestly at the Final Four news conference. "It is just so much fun for me to be here, and I almost didn't get here. But I fought hard enough to do that because I wanted to be with the guys."

Three months after the Ramblers' improbable run to the Final Four, I asked Sister Jean how the increased fame has affected her daily life.

"It has changed my life a lot. It hasn't changed my prayer life at all. But it has changed my life otherwise," she said. "I can't let it go to my head. I do as much as I can do for my congregation and for Loyola and for the Missouri Valley and the city of Chicago and the nation. That is what I want to do. If I can make people happy, make them believe more in God and get closer to God, that's fine."

Sister Jean relied on the assistance of Loyola assistant athletic director Bill Behrns to help her stay organized amid all the increased media and fan attention.

"I have so much mail coming in—email, snail mail—telling me how wonderful it was," she said. "Perhaps other people are grasping the whole thing better than I am. The first day I was in Dallas, I got up the next morning and said to myself, 'Wow! This is surreal. This is not a dream. So you better shape up here.' I have been on a roll ever since. I have done a lot of interviews with different people. And I really don't know how this all burst so quickly. But it did. People say to me, 'Well, what do you do about it?' And I say that I just go with the flow."

Special presentations and recognitions followed Sister Jean when she returned to Chicago. She was asked to throw out a ceremonial first pitch before the Chicago Cubs home opener against the Pirates at Wrigley Field in 2018. Moser and guard Ben Richardson joined her in throwing out ceremonial pitches. She accompanied Moser to Springfield, Illinois, for state Senate recognition. And other Chicago-area organizations have saluted her as well.

"They were taking pictures and asking questions and I said, 'I am not Princess Diana, but I have paparazzi all around me all the time.' And if it makes people happy, that's what counts," she said with a laugh.

Letters and news clippings came pouring in from all over the world—Germany, Mexico, South America, Central America, as well as the United States.

"Some of the letters are very emotional and very touching," she told me. "I do appreciate those. One man told me that he had been away from his faith and church beliefs for 40 years and that he was going back to church on Easter Sunday. So that really touched me."

Sister Jean was born in San Francisco on Aug. 21, 1919, and has never forgotten her roots. Neither have her friends, especially after her burgeoning celebrity.

"I heard from someone I lived next door to in San Francisco. She is five years younger than I, but we grew up together," she said. "And I heard from someone I taught in my very first class here in Chicago at St. Vincent's grade school. I taught her in fifth grade in 1940. Her son knew that his mother went there, so he followed it through with a call to Bill

Behrns, and sure enough I had taught her in the fifth grade. We talked on the phone and that was good. And I have heard from people in California that I taught more than 60 years ago in eighth grade. And I heard from a lot of alums from Loyola.

"It has been real enriching to get those phone calls because it brings back happy memories. It has been a real gift of faith for me because people I don't know have sent me emails and talked about their faith. Or I see people here at Loyola and they say how great it was to hear me talk about God, and I say, 'Well, I am not afraid to talk about Him.' And neither is Porter. He talks about God and prayer. And it is not just something we put on because we are being interviewed. It comes from our heart. And it is part of us to do that with our students. I think that helps with the faith of our students."

Moser has witnessed the tangible influence Sister Jean has had on his players and his program.

"Well before she became an international celebrity, as she puts it, she was like our comfort blanket," Moser said. "We would see Sister Jean around and we would pray with her before games. You would walk by the student center and her door is always open and you pop in. And she is not only like the comfort blanket to our team, she has been the comfort blanket for the whole campus. You would see nonathletes in there talking to her all the time. You spend a couple of minutes with her and you just feel better. She's got that presence, that smile. She always seems to have the right thing to say. In my profession as a coach, when you win, then everyone wants to be your friend. If you lose, you've got the Scarlet Letter on you. And Sister Jean emails you after every game. Win or lose. And she will email the players. It might be just two lines, like, 'Hey, we'll get 'em next time.' Or, 'We'll get the Salukis next time.'

"But she will send an email after every game to each player and to each coach. Just those one or two lines of encouragement, knowing that someone was thinking about you in a positive light after a loss...that's when you know someone is all-in. It just isn't when you win. She cares about Loyola."

Dr. Tom Hitcho, Loyola's senior associate athletic director and longest tenured employee in the department, was tasked with pushing Sister Jean around in a wheelchair during the 2018 NCAA Tournament. It became a labor of love.

"It was an honor to be with her. She is an inspiration. It was a once-in-a-lifetime opportunity," Hitcho told me. "She said she would do it all over again. She had such a good time."

Sister Jean would have generally moved about energetically without the aid of a wheelchair. At her 95th birthday celebration, then-Loyola President Father Michael Garanzini presented her with a new pair of running shoes. On the back of her left shoe reads "Sister" and on the heel of the right shoe reads "Jean."

So it was not normal to see her being wheeled around during the 2018 NCAA Tournament.

"She fell and had a hip replacement and she had surgery. That's why she was in the wheelchair," said Hitcho, a member of Loyola's Athletic Hall of Fame.

Her lack of mobility did not limit the amount of pleasure she derived from the tournament experience.

"She enjoyed meeting the celebrities like Charles Barkley and Bill Walton. The NCAA was so supportive. With Sister Jean, it was always, 'You tell us what you need' from the NCAA," Hitcho said.

Hitcho was not totally surprised that Sister Jean had such a major impact internationally during the Final Four.

"Here at Loyola, this is something we have known all of this time," he said. "She has been our treasure all of this time. Now we are able to share her. We still get calls from people saying she is such an inspiration. Because of the NCAA Tournament, she has been exposed to the nation and the international media as well. So it is a treasure that we have and have been able to share. She has been an inspiration, considering what the NCAA basketball has been going through. She was such an appropriate story, a good story."

Hitcho's long affiliation with the Loyola basketball program is especially worth noting. "I was George Ireland's last hire in '77. I was the athletic trainer and the assistant to the athletic director," he said. "So after three or four months, he had some health issues and we had an interim athletic director, a Jesuit. Father Riley. And then the following year Gene Sullivan became the AD. Prior to that he had been at DePaul."

Ireland had coached the Ramblers to the NCAA title in 1963. An All-American basketball player at Notre Dame in the 1930s, Ireland died in 2001 at 88.

Hitcho, a Duquesne, Pennsylvania, native who completed his undergraduate studies at Youngstown State University, was a trainer and graduate student studying sports medicine at Indiana State University before coming to Loyola, where he earned a Ph.D. in 1996. He has observed significant changes at Loyola over the decades.

"The university has always been a very good academic school. It used to be more of a commuter school," he said. "Now there is not only the Lakeshore campus, but the Water Tower campus and the medical center. Now it is more of a national university. When I first started here, we had water polo and women's sports were just starting. Gene Sullivan was an advocate for that."

Sullivan had been DePaul's athletic director from 1975 to 1978. He then became AD at Loyola before becoming the school's basketball coach in 1980. Sullivan's 1985 Ramblers squad, led by Alfredrick Hughes, advanced to the NCAA Tournament Sweet 16. Sullivan, who left Loyola in 1989, had a record of 149–114. He died in 2002 at 70.

Hughes is Loyola's all-time leading scorer with 2,914 points. He averaged 27.6 points as a junior and 26.3 points as a senior. He scored a school-record 47 points in a game against Detroit in 1985. Following his collegiate career, Hughes' jersey No. 21 was retired by Loyola.

Hughes announced after his junior year that he would forgo the NBA draft and play his senior year at Loyola. After that he became a first-round draft pick of the San Antonio Spurs in 1985, the 14th overall selection.

His NBA career lasted just one year after averaging 5.2 points in 68 games. He went on to play in the Italian League and for a variety of non-NBA teams throughout the United States.

The Loyola experience involves far more than athletics.

All current and former Loyola students and athletes have been taught the mission of the university.

For instance, Hitcho said he remains eternally grateful to the Society of Jesus, or Jesuits, and Saint Ignatius for their mission to serve those in need and to become compassionate persons for others.

"I feel this is an integral part of the student transformation process and culture for the success of our student-athletes on the court and in the classroom," he said.

Perhaps that is why Sister Jean's presence on campus has translated so well when it comes to the intersection of sports and spirituality on the Loyola campus.

So how did this affable 99-year-old nun capture the attention of an entire nation?

"I keep asking myself that question too," Sister Jean said. "First of all, this is something that Porter, his team, and his assistants have achieved. I have not achieved the Final Four. I was appointed as their chaplain. But I think it is because I am a sister and because I am (99) years old.... I think that has a lot to do with it. Even during the Missouri Valley playoffs, the announcer said, 'Today, Sister Jean is up there in the balcony.'

"And I am not afraid to talk about God. People like to hear that and also believe in God."

Sister Jean's fascination with the sport of basketball also captured the attention of her fans and colleagues.

"As for my community (of nuns), they had watch parties all over the country, which is unusual," she said. "And a group of sisters are starting their own basketball team. I have been with the (Loyola) team since 1994, at the old gymnasium as well as the new."

Hitcho said he marveled particularly at the way Sister Jean dealt with the swarming media during the tournament run.

"She really did well with Coy Wire of CNN. They really hit it off well," Hitcho said. "And before the interview, Coy goes, 'Sister, I have interviewed superstars...but I am nervous.'

"She said, 'That's all right, I will help you.'

"She always has a sense of humor. She never says no for an interview or a picture. And she will do whatever she can for a Loyola alum, whether it is a student or parent."

Loyola players are not reluctant to talk about Sister Jean and the genuine impact she has had on their lives on and off the court. During the NCAA Tournament they were asked as many questions about her as they were about sinking the winning baskets.

And when the Ramblers' quest for a national champion-ship finally ended with the tough loss to Michigan, Sister Jean was there to offer emotional support to the Loyola players.

"People asked me how I felt when they came off the court. I say that I felt the same way they did, that we were fortunate to get to the Final Four," she said. "And through tears and sweaty bodies, the players said, 'Next year, Number One.' I think they bounced back pretty quickly because they have a wonderful spirit."

The combination of extensive travel, exhilarating games and a ramped-up schedule was enough to test a person half the age of Sister Jean.

"When I went to Dallas and San Antonio and Atlanta, people said, 'How do you do all that?' I said, 'I don't know.' But when that was all over, I was tired," she admitted.

As we all grow older, it is not uncommon to focus more on our legacy. What do we want people to remember about us when we are gone? Sister Jean was quick with her response when I asked.

"I want people to say that I brought God into people's lives. And that I led a good life," she said. "And for my community, I want to always do what is best for my community and for wherever I work. I am at Loyola now and I am part of Loyola and the campus ministry. And I also claim athletics. And that came almost by default because I was simply asked in 1994 to work with the team by the president. So I felt that was bona fide."

Sister Jean was around the Loyola team during the lean years as well as the Final Four finish in 2018.

"I believe that being in the Missouri Valley has helped us so much," she said. "It was a great thing that we applied and a great thing that Father Garanzini agreed to do this. We were good in the Horizon League, but sometimes we played down to other teams. We didn't have the right mind-set. When we got into the Valley, we realized what it was like. When you go through change in life, you have to go through what we call in Catholicism 'the passion and the depth and the resurrection.' You have to go through those three stages. And I have tried to fit that into our basketball."

Sister Jean, as always, was able to relate her abiding faith to the trials of playing college basketball.

"So as I look through our history in the Missouri Valley, the first year, I think we were scared," she said very frankly. "We knew they were good and we knew that Creighton had moved out. But we knew that Wichita State was really good. So I put that with the passion. We played basketball passionately, but not well enough.

"Then the next thing is the whole thing of crucifixion and suffering. So the next year they put us down; they were better than we were. Then the resurrection...this is it. We have come a long way in the four years we have been in the Valley. But the Valley has inspired us to work as hard as we can. And that is why I use the slogan to 'Worship, Work and Win.' The three Ws.

"And that is what everyone has to do," she said. "You have to pray, you have to work, and winning comes out of that. When you have a job, you win too. You may be working in the mail room for a while, but you will get up there if you work hard."

A long-standing ritual before Loyola basketball games includes Sister Jean leading the players in prayer privately. Then she grabs the microphone and leads the crowd in prayer before home games at Gentile Arena.

Donte Ingram said he was surprised initially to hear Sister Jean provide game instructions after offering a team prayer.

"With our teams, we do pray. I make a different prayer for every game," she said. "We pray together in the huddle. My prayer isn't always very holy because I give them some pointers at that time. I have scouted and I will tell them who they should watch out for. Porter will talk to them first, but a lot of times Porter and I are on the same page. And he doesn't mind that I do that."

Sister Jean is not bashful when it comes to giving advice to opposing coaches and referees as well.

"One time, the opponent's coach was at the scorer's table and he was starting to write down his starters. So I turned to him and said, 'Would you like for me to fill them in for you?'" she said.

"He said, 'Sure, do that.' So I wrote down the names and the numbers on the chart. I said, 'The No. 5 player is on you.' So I wrote down the first four and that was a fun thing for me. Because he had the same names written down."

Sister Jean has been such an integral part of the basketball team's routine.

"I know our players count on the prayer," she said. "And I pray with fans before we sing the 'Star-Spangled Banner.' And that one (prayer) is different. I look at the history of the team we are playing and I pray that we don't have any injuries on either team. That we do what we have been taught and that we are good sports. Also, God, help us make those baskets so that the scoreboard will say that we get the big 'W.'

"And I pray that the referees will look at it very cheerfully. And sometimes when I see them on the court, I ask them how their eyesight is. A couple of times, they will ask me to go to their locker room to pray with them, which I have done. It thrills me that we do those things."

With so many last-second shots determining Loyola's victories during the 2018 NCAA Tournament, Sister Jean's emotions were supremely tested.

"The team knows also that when the game gets close I will pray to myself. I tell them I will have to take my nitroglycerin pretty soon," she said with a laugh.

Sister Jean was just 43 years old when the 1963 Loyola men's basketball team shocked the world by upsetting Cincinnati to win the NCAA title.

"I have to say that I think there is a similarity between the 1963 team and this team," Sister Jean said. "The similarity comes in the unselfish play and generous playing. Because the end of that 1963 game was true unselfishness. And if a team can catch up 20 points in a game, you know they had to share the ball. One person could not do that."

Sister Jean also made note of the uniform fashion differences over the decades.

"Even though they looked different in shorter shorts...I think the shorts today are more comfortable for them. I haven't heard them complain about them," she said.

But emphasis on sportsmanship and religion has not changed at Loyola over the years.

"The 1963 team...those fellows prayed too. I don't think they had a chaplain, but I know that they prayed," she said. "They were good and they had a great team spirit. Same as this team. I am calling the 1963 team 'The Game Changer One' and this team is 'Game Changer Two.' Because they brought a new culture here. These two teams brought universal basketball. You could see on their faces that they really enjoyed playing the games."

Part of the beauty of Loyola basketball has been that entire families are engaged and impacted positively.

"I have never seen mothers more united to their young sons. And they are such a wonderful group together, encouraging each other to go to the games. And they travel," Sister Jean said.

Another positive change in the Loyola basketball program has been a greater emphasis on academic success.

"When I first came into the program of athletics, some of the young men and women had kind of shaky grade-point averages. The president said they could use our encouragement," she said. "So I had those students come see me once a week so that I could look at their work and see how they were progressing and see if they had their assignments ready and everything."

Sister Jean has been known to hand out prayer cards during finals week and ride with students on the school shuttles. She also has kept up with social media.

Loyola conferred upon Sister Jean an honorary Doctor of Humane Letters degree in 2016.

But all of the recent accolades bring back the long-ago experiences of her youth.

Sister Jean retains vivid memories of her days growing up in the Eureka Valley area of San Francisco.

"I had a very happy childhood," she said. "I had two brothers and a mom and dad who were just there for us all the time. When we weren't right we were corrected and when we were right we were praised. That was a good feeling. I think of that often when I watch Porter on the court. If a young man has made a mistake, he pulls him out, tells him what the mistake is and tries to correct it. Then he puts him back in so that the young man feels good because he is not out for the whole game. I feel that was kind of how my mom and dad kind of worked with us too.

"We had fun. We always had to do our homework first. And then we went out to play. We had no television, no telephones. We had a party-line phone during the Depression, but we had to have it taken out because it cost like 5 cents a call. But we weren't calling our friends all the time anyway. We saw our friends at school and then we would play with our neighborhood friends. Some went to a Catholic school, some went to a private school. And some went to a public school. So we all played together. We played games like One Foot Off the Gutter and Red Light, Red Light, and Kick the Can."

Sister Jean was determined to keep up with her brothers while growing up.

"We did ride bicycles, but San Francisco is so hilly and there wasn't that much opportunity," she said. "We rode mainly in our neighborhood and we were at the top of the hill. My brothers and I went to a Catholic school. I went to a public school my first year because my mother was pregnant with my little brother. In those days, little kids didn't know about being pregnant. We just said we were going to find a baby in the park or in the tree."

Concerns about her safety consumed her parents when she was young when it came to the busy streets of San Francisco.

"There are, like, six intersections in San Francisco on Market Street where I would have had to cross. And my mother was afraid of cars because there were no stoplights there," she said. "Cars just made their own rules. Then I went to Catholic school the next year. I had a lay sister because they were short of sisters at that time."

Sister Jean realized at a very early age that she wanted to become a nun.

"In third grade our teacher said we were not too young to think about what God wanted us to do," she recalled. "And talk to God every day about what He thinks we should do. I always thought that was pretty neat. She actually was telling us—in the words that we use today—not to let anyone squelch our dreams. We need to do what we believe we need to do. If we don't, then we might be unhappy all of our lives. At that time there were not many options for young girls. We would never think of being a doctor or a lawyer or work in the police department. We had to be like secretaries, teachers or a stay-at-home mother. I knew I wanted to be a teacher; we had teachers on both sides of our family. But then I knew we had sisters on both sides of our family.

"I used to say to God, 'Please let me be a sister. But tell me you want me to be a BVM sister.' That is Blessed Virgin Mary. And that is the kind I am now. So that is what attracted me to the BVM. And I went to a BVM high school. To get a scholarship to St. Paul's, you had to have the highest grade-point in the class. And I got that."

Sister Jean also developed an early appreciation for the game of basketball, playing on the high school team before graduating in 1937.

"In California we (girls) only played indoor basketball in tournaments. Otherwise we played outdoors on the tarmac. It was a real transition to play indoors," she said. "Like the girls play quarters and the boys have halves. I hope the boys never go to quarters because they would lose their momentum."

At 18 and armed with just one suitcase, Sister Jean boarded a train to Dubuque, Iowa, where she entered the convent of the Sisters of Charity of the Blessed Virgin Mary to become a nun.

She received a bachelor's degree from Mount St. Mary's College in Los Angeles in 1949, and a master's degree from Loyola of Los Angeles (now Loyola Marymount) in 1961.

She taught elementary school and coached girls basketball, volleyball and track in Los Angeles, North Hollywood and Chicago.

In 1961, she began teaching at Mundelein College in the Rogers Park neighborhood of Chicago. When Mundelein College was merged into Loyola of Chicago in 1991, Sister Jean was hired by Loyola. She was honored with a "Sister Jean Day" in 2012.

As a sports fan, even as a young child, Sister Jean and her friends and family closely followed Notre Dame football and the team's legendary coach Knute Rockne. In their mind, Notre Dame played the quintessential form of college football.

But on March 31, 1931, Rockne died in a plane crash in Bazaar, Kan., at the age of 43. Sister Jean was 11 at the time.

Rockne had grown up in Chicago's Logan Square neighborhood and attended North West Division High School. He worked in a post office as a mail dispatcher for four years before enrolling at Notre Dame at 22 and becoming an All-American end on the football team. He graduated in 1914 with a degree in pharmacy and later played professionally with the Akron Pros and Massillon Tigers. Rockne's greatest renown came from coaching Notre Dame for 13 years to a record of 105–12–5 and three national championships.

Rockne died in the plane crash while heading to Kansas for the production of a film—*The Spirit of Notre Dame*. He had stopped in Kansas City to visit his two sons, who were in boarding school there. About an hour after takeoff, the plane crashed in a wheat field, killing Rockne and seven other passengers.

"When Knute Rockne was killed, I was at my grandma's house for lunch," Sister Jean recalled vividly. "And my uncle always had the radio on. He came home for lunch, so I heard that Knute Rockne died. When I went back to school, I told all the kids at the playground. They said, 'Go tell the sisters, because they don't listen to the radio.'

"So I went to ring the bell to tell the sisters that Knute Rockne had been killed. They said, 'Thank you for telling us that. We will pray for him. You should too.'

"I just thought that was a great response."

On Aug. 21, 2018, Sister Jean celebrated her 99th birthday. A contingent of Loyola University staff, administrators and students was invited to take part in the ceremony in the Damen Center of the university.

Sister Jean, who had not been feeling very well at the time, appeared energized by the outpouring of affection and appreciation.

"There were times when I thought I would never live this long," she said. "When I was looking forward to the year 2000, I said, 'Wow! This is something. I have crossed the 1900s and into 2000.' And now that I have made it this far, I hope to see all of you next year. Except the seniors, of course. I want you to graduate. God bless you and know that we are all Ramblers and we always will be a Rambler."

Cardinal Blase Cupich offered a video salute to Sister Jean during the ceremony.

Moser handed her a specially made Loyola basketball jersey with No. 99 inscribed on it.

"The one thing you notice is that she is 99. But she has done her vocation for 80 years," Moser said off to the side after the formal part of the ceremony. "That is truly amazing that someone could do their vocation for 80 years. And doing it the way she is doing it.

"Going through coaching, they always tell you, it's not how many wins or losses you accumulate. It's the lives you impact. That's what people remember. And people will remember the impact she has had on so many lives. That's what is really cool, to see her wit, her energy at 99 years old. And I have no doubt we will be here again a year from today."

Moser has been able to witness Sister Jean's methods both on and off the basketball court.

"The thing that the whole country saw...they see her in a wheelchair. That's not how we see her," he said. "She just had an accident. Before the accident in the fall, she was boogying around campus, through the ice and everywhere. She is a high-energy, self-sufficient, very bright, energetic, loving, compassionate woman. And it is so fun to see her impact, and for the whole country to see that."

Moser projected what he believes will be the legacy of Sister Jean.

"Her undying spirit...she has just got a spirit about herself," he said. "You can be walking around and having a bad day and all of a sudden you are around her and you just can't help but smile. She is always smiling. Even through the mayhem of the media circus that happened with her, she still just had that funny, sweet, calm demeanor. And she has that presence. She has an amazing spiritual presence about her."

The incoming Loyola basketball players knew all about Sister Jean, well before joining their teammates.

"We had three incoming freshmen this summer that already knew," Moser said. "I mean, we introduced her to the recruits on their visit. So she is part of our recruiting visit. It's not an act. The upperclassmen don't even have to talk to them. She just naturally invites you into her world. And it is a natural process when the new students come on to this campus...she is just so welcoming. There isn't an educational process."

Moser, who grew up receiving a Catholic education, joked when asked how Sister Jean is different from the nuns who taught him in grade school.

"She doesn't have a ruler in her hand," he said with a laugh. "My knuckles always seem good around her. I don't have any ruler marks on my knuckles. She is all good."

Moser remembers meeting Sister Jean for the first time when he was introduced at the news conference to announce his hiring.

"I was in my office and there was a folder on my desk. And I opened it up, and when I opened it up it was a letter from her," he said. "And the letter included each returning player and what their strengths and weaknesses are. It was fun to read through it and see her take on it."

Sophomore forward Lucas Williamson recalled interacting with Sister Jean during his freshman year at Loyola.

"She has so much energy for her age, and just being around her is like a blessing," Williamson said. "We definitely cherish every moment we share with her."

The uniqueness of having a nun being such an integral part of the basketball program is not considered out of the ordinary at Loyola.

"It's just something special," Williamson said. "Last year being my freshman year, and then meeting her for the first time, it was like, 'OK, this is something special we have going on here.' She has been our biggest fan, whether we are winning or losing. We're just so lucky to have her."

The emails that Sister Jean sends out to players and coaches provide inspiration for the recipients of all ages.

"It means a lot," said Williamson. "She is just like another coach. Before every game, she knows what the other team's best players are. She gives us her own scouting report. She is just a very special lady."

Every year that Moser has coached at Loyola, Sister Jean has had the team gather around at the first practice of the fall and given them a blessing.

"My first year, I remember Sister Jean saying, 'We want to worship, work...'—and then I could just feel her hand gouge into my back—'and win!'"

On Oct. 12, 2018, Sister Jean was inducted into the Illinois Senior Hall of Fame during ceremonies at Loyola University that included Illinois Gov. Bruce Rauner, state Sen. John Cullerton and acting Loyola provost Dr. Margaret Callahan. Cullerton, the Illinois Senate president who happens to be a Loyola alumnus, nominated Sister Jean for the special recognition.

"When I saw that the Department of Aging was taking nominations for its Senior Hall of Fame, to me I thought it was pretty obvious," Cullerton said. "Who better than Sister Jean? It's not just because I am a double Loyola alum (also a law school graduate) looking out for a fellow Rambler, although that would be perfectly fine and legitimate. And it is not just because the men's basketball team went to the Final Four, as much fun as that was. The world has come to know and love Sister Jean thanks to the team's magical run in the NCAA Tournament. She added a fascinating chapter to that wonderful story.

"Along the way, she became a goodwill ambassador for our school, our city and our state. And it's kind of like we let the rest of the world catch a glimpse of the guiding light that Sister Jean has long shown. But honestly, Sister Jean is deserving of this award, even if Loyola had never won a game. Although, thank God, they did. She is a fixture within the university's community."

Sister Jean was one of four individuals added to the Senior Hall of Fame in 2018. The Hall of Fame was established in 1994 by the General Assembly to honor and recognize the contributions of Illinoisans 65 and over.

Cullerton heaped well-deserved praise on Sister Jean for the work she has done over many decades.

"She has opened doors to nontraditional students, worked to expand higher education for immigrants, united generations and has served as a daily emissary and counselor to the greater student body, faculty, staff and neighborhood," Cullerton said. "Through her devotion and diligence, she has expanded and diversified education in Illinois, while remaining attentive and attuned to the students, whoever they might be.

"In the '60s, she was active in the civil rights movement. In the '70s, she helped establish policies to ensure fairness during the student strike. More recently, she has been honored with not one, but two bobblehead dolls. Frankly, Sister Jean, I am stunned that no one so far has mentioned you for mayor," he added with a smile.

"The simple fact that Sister Jean has lived a life of service and has made this institution forever better...she has worked as a daily inspiration for thousands of current and future students. It's for all of those reasons and many, many more that I nominated Sister Jean for this recognition."

Sister Jean sat in her wheelchair near the podium and humbly listened to the many words of praise.

"I am very honored to receive this award for education in the Department of Aging," Sister Jean told the assembled media and well-wishers. "And to be inducted into the Illinois Hall of Fame...I just get so emotional when I get these awards when I hear all of these wonderful things about myself. And it is sort of a review of my life, as it were. And I think to myself, 'Oh, yes, I did that.' It's kind of nice. And so often I say to myself, 'I wish I could go back to an earlier age because there is so much going on today and I am going to miss out so much.'

"It's just like when my grandnephew was 8, he would tell his mother, 'You know, Mom, I don't think I am going to live to see and do all that I want to do in my life.' And she got real nervous about that too. He's about 35 now and he is having a very good life, learning all things. And I would like to say that is what I am doing too."

Gov. Rauner also expressed his appreciation for the countless good deeds Sister Jean has done in her lifetime.

"Sister Jean represents everything that is wonderful in life," Rauner said. "Faith, love of community, love of

God. Giving back to those most vulnerable among us. Sister Jean...teacher, advisor, coach, civil rights advocate. The true meaning of a wonderful life, serving the Lord, serving our fellow human beings."

Sister Jean deferred some of the credit for all the personal adulation she has received.

"It humbles me to receive this award because I think of it as something that not just I earned," she said. "It's a team effort. Because throughout my life, my family, my Loyola community...all of these wonderful people...the governor, Sen. Cullerton, the selection committee and the whole Department of Aging...I am so grateful to you. As I look at this award, I think of all the seniors who are coming up and getting older. Every one of us is getting older every day. We have to say that although we don't like to hear it.

"I just want to tell every one of you to work until you actually want to stop. You really never should stop. Because when you stop, that's the end of the line in my way of thinking. We can always do more.

"We can always do good by a smile, or goodness in some way or other," Sister Jean said. "It pleases me when I see people my age or even older. Someone sent me a video yesterday of a man celebrating his 110th birthday. And she sent a little email to me: 'Don't you feel young, Sister Jean?'

"I don't feel too much younger than that, but it thrills me to see people who are continuing to do things. So we really never get too old to do things. Age is just a number. And someone asked me: 'How come you are so generous in telling people your age?'

"Women are so hesitant about telling their age. But once you get to one spot and announce it, that's the end. So just keep on adding the years."

Sister Jean also spoke again about the magnificent 2018 Final Four team that gained the admiration of so many across the country.

"They are the most wonderful group of young men," she said. "They are very passionate about what they do. They wanted it so badly, and I could see it in their faces as they came off the court. I had so many favorite moments during the whole March Madness. I think everything was a very special moment, especially when we made those big baskets that could have popped either in or out.

"The coach is great, and they learn more than just basketball. And I am just delighted by how much joy we brought to the world, and we hope to do that. So we ask your prayers that God will help us do what we need to do this season.

"And, of course, I have to say: Go Ramblers!"

On Nov. 17, 2018, Sister Jean was recognized in St. Louis with a Stan Musial Award for her humanitarian service.

She was given her own Final Four ring on Nov. 27, 2018, when Loyola athletic director Steve Watson made the presentation prior to the Ramblers' regular-season contest against the University of Nevada at Gentile Arena.

"I'll probably gain five pounds by having this on my finger now," Sister Jean quipped when interviewed by sportscaster Lou Canellis of Fox-32 Chicago. "It is nice to have it presented in front of this big crowd. They are the ones who helped get it."

1963 National Champs!

The year 1963 was both groundbreaking and unsettling in America on so many fronts—social reform, political upheaval, racial confrontation, cultural renaissance... and certainly in the Chicago area, unprecedented athletic achievement.

In so many ways, times then were very different than they are today. The average cost of a new house then was $12,650. The average family income was $5,807. A new car cost $3,233. And a gallon of gas was 29 cents.

Michael Jordan was born Feb. 17, 1963. Who knew then what he would become? The Beatles released their first album that year. And the system of ZIP codes was implemented in the United States. Dr. Martin Luther King Jr. delivered his powerful and poignant "I Have A Dream" speech. James Meredith became the first African-American to graduate from the University of Mississippi. And, horrifically, members of the

Ku Klux Klan bombed a Baptist church in Birmingham, Ala., killing four young black girls.

In the 10 weeks before Dr. King's famous speech, there had been 758 demonstrations in 186 cities resulting in 14,733 arrests, according to the U.S. Justice Department.

In Chicago, civil unrest and tensions were brewing in 1963, but it wasn't until 1966 and '68 that riots broke out following Dr. King's planned march through the segregated Marquette Park neighborhood. In 1968, riots erupted on the West Side of Chicago following the assassination of Dr. King. Over 600 protesters and 152 police officers were injured during the Democratic National Convention in late August.

On Nov. 22, 1963, president John F. Kennedy was assassinated in Dallas, Texas, rocking the nation to this day. On Dec. 29, 1963, the Chicago Bears defeated the New York Giants, 14–10, at Wrigley Field to win the National Football League championship game, which predated the Super Bowl in those days as the ultimate testament of superiority in professional football.

On March 23, 1963, the Loyola Ramblers made history at Freedom Hall in Louisville, Kentucky, by winning the NCAA men's basketball championship with a dramatic 60–58 overtime comeback victory over the two-time defending national champion Cincinnati Bearcats.

The famous call from former legendary DePaul broadcaster Red Rush:

"Harkness going inside the lane. Now he goes back out to Miller. Fifteen seconds. Out to Egan. I guarantee you one thing. They'll give it to Harkness when it's time. Miller's got it. Out to Rouse. Nine, eight. Harkness has got it. Here he goes. He jumps. He passes off to Hunter.

"Hunter shoots, hitting off the rim. Rouse tips it, scores! It's over! It's over! We won! We won! We won! We won the ballgame! We won the ballgame! We won! Loyola won the ballgame! Ohhh, we won it! We won, 60 to 58!"

Rush was an unapologetic "homer" who would hype one of the station's bread sponsors by saying "Gonella is swella, fella." He would refer to a close game as a "ding-dong dilly of a ballgame." And of course, he would say a shot "tickled the twines" or "swisheroo" for a DePaul basket.

Rush also did play-by-play for several Major League Baseball teams: the White Sox, Oakland A's and St. Louis Cardinals. He called Loyola basketball games from the early '60s to the late '80s. In addition, Rush, whose real first name was Wresley, announced Northwestern football games, and games for the Minneapolis Lakers and Golden State Warriors. He died on Jan. 11, 2009 at 81.

Led by coach George Ireland, Loyola became the first NCAA men's major college basketball team to feature four African-American starters. With Cincinnati starting three black players, seven of the 10 starters in the NCAA title game were African-American.

Former Loyola forward Les Hunter told me that Ireland was reluctant at first to start so many black players for the 1962–63 season.

"Once he did, I think he was glad he did, because it resulted in a championship," Hunter said. "For him to all of a sudden come up with all of these black guys and just beat the heck out of these teams...they really were livid. There were altercations right on the court at the end of games toward him because he came in with the black guys and was beating teams by 30 points and 50 points."

I was 15 in 1963 and immediately became keenly aware of the significance of all those events. I watched the initial newscast and video accompanying Kennedy's assassination on a tiny black-and-white TV in the kitchen of my friend Reginald Hayes' house. On a Friday afternoon, Reggie and I and another classmate, Hancy Jones, had been eating lunch at Hayes' house before heading back to school for afternoon classes during our junior year of high school.

Kennedy was declared dead at 1 p.m., CST. Lee Harvey Oswald was arrested and charged with the murder of our 35th president. Then two days later on live TV, much of America watched Oswald being shot by Dallas nightclub owner Jack Ruby while police attempted to transport Oswald from their headquarters to the Dallas County Jail.

Lyndon Johnson was thrust into the role as president of the United States as social unrest in America was coupled with mounting tension in Vietnam.

The specter of young men being drafted and sent to fight and perhaps die in the Vietnam War was daunting and somewhat terrifying. It was an unpopular war and so many of our friends would lose their lives in Vietnam. Yet social unrest here in America further complicated matters, particularly for minorities.

By 1963, Cassius Clay, who became Muhammad Ali in 1964, already had amassed a record of 19–0, including 15 wins by knockout. And he had become as much renowned for his anti-war rhetoric as his boxing prowess. Just four years later, 1967, Ali infuriated much of the establishment by refusing to be drafted as a conscientious objector for religious reasons as a member of the Nation of Islam.

Music, sports, politics…there certainly was a lot to discuss at the barber shops across America in 1963.

I also had a firsthand look at the Chicago Bears' 1963 championship game that my father took me to watch on a frigid afternoon by the lakefront. We were among 45,801 fans in attendance and our tickets cost $12.50 each. We sat in the east stands of the ballpark as the brutal wind singed our faces during an era that predated wind-chill factor calculations. I had worn a pair of long underwear, two pairs of sweat socks under my winter boots, a pair of gloves, a scarf and a sweater under my hooded winter coat. Yet I still froze like I never have to this day.

I had the opportunity to interview former Bears halfback Ronnie Bull years later and I asked him about playing in that 1963 game.

"The turf was in pretty good shape when we started. It was solidly frozen when we finished," Bull said. "The worst part of it was when you left the bench and the heaters and took off those big, heavy parkas and went on the field. Then they would say 'TV timeout' and you are just standing there for five minutes or so with that wind blowing.

"And I didn't wear gloves. (George) Halas really didn't want us wearing gloves. Some of the offensive linemen snuck out gloves, but Halas didn't believe in that kind of stuff. All I had on was a tear-away jersey and a T-shirt underneath. Once your adrenaline gets going, you don't notice it. The one thing you had to watch out for was when you caught a pass that you didn't catch it on the seams. The seams would injure your hands."

Each player on the winning Bears team was paid $6,000. In contrast, each member of the Philadelphia Eagles earned $112,000 for winning last season's Super Bowl. That was in addition to earning $79,000 each for winning the previous two rounds of the playoffs. Not a bad bonus payday.

On the national level, 1963 was the first year of the Pro Football Hall of Fame in Canton, Ohio. There were 17 charter members. The initial inductees were: Sammy Baugh, Bert Bell, Joe Carr, Earl "Dutch" Clark, Harold "Red" Grange, George Halas, Mel Hein, Wilbur "Pete" Henry, Robert "Cal" Hubbard, Don Hutson, Earl "Curly" Lambeau, John "Blood" McNally, Tim Mara, George Preston Marshall, Bronko Nagurski, Ernie Nevers and Jim Thorpe.

In college football, Roger Staubach of Navy was the Heisman Trophy winner. And instant replay was used on television for the first time during the 1963 Army-Navy football game.

The Los Angeles Dodgers swept the Yankees 4–0 in the World Series as pitcher Sandy Koufax claimed the series MVP award. The Boston Celtics outlasted the Los Angeles Lakers four games to two to capture the NBA title. And on July 22, 1963, Sonny Liston knocked out Floyd Patterson in the first round to win the heavyweight boxing title.

The Toronto Maple Leafs defeated the Detroit Red Wings four games to one to take home the Stanley Cup. And Jack Nicklaus won the 1963 Masters, although Arnold Palmer finished as the PGA Tour money winner with $128,230.

Loyola's NCAA basketball championship also took on personal significance to me and my family that year. I watched that game on a black-and-white TV as well, not knowing at the time that it was being shown on tape delay. There was no social media at that time to spoil the excitement of watching the Ramblers pull off one of the biggest upsets in college basketball history.

My father, LeRoy Mitchell Jr., was a University of Cincinnati alumnus and a devoted fan of the entire athletic program. My uncle, Austin Tillotson, and favorite aunt, Gladys Tillotson, were deeply involved in the Bearcats' basketball program, especially since they had no kids of their own. They took in the great Oscar Robertson to live with them during his freshman year at U.C. Then they did the same for All-American George Wilson.

I was 13 or 14 at the time I first got to meet them and I really looked up to the 6–5 Robertson and 6–8 Wilson, literally and figuratively. Robertson, of course, went on to become a Hall of Fame guard in the NBA and arguably one of the greatest NBA players of all-time. Wilson, who led Marshall High School in Chicago to two state titles, won an NCAA title with the Bearcats in 1962 and a gold medal for the United States in the Summer Olympics of 1964 before experiencing a relatively modest NBA career, averaging 5.4 points and 5.2 rebounds.

Wilson played with the Cincinnati Royals, Seattle Super-Sonics, Phoenix Suns, Philadelphia 76ers and Buffalo Braves.

"I was the player everybody wanted but nobody wanted to keep," Wilson once told me. In 2010, Wilson, now a YMCA director in Ohio, was inducted into the Ohio Basketball Hall of Fame.

Loyola's spectacular win over Cincinnati in 1963 concluded with a tip-in by Vic Rouse following a missed shot. Rouse's game-winner came over the outstretched arm of Wilson. To perhaps exacerbate my father's frustration of seeing his alma mater knocked off in the national championship game came the fact that Rouse would later intern under him when my father worked as a labor relations executive at Inland Steel Co. in East Chicago, Ind.

It became a bit of a running joke between the two of them as that last-second shot was relived. My father had great respect for Rouse, however, and was proud to see his career unfold. Rouse, a 6–7 forward, was selected in the seventh round of the 1964 NBA draft by the Cincinnati Royals, but he never played in the league. He did, however, go on to earn three master's degrees and a Ph.D. He owned his own consulting firm and taught courses at the University of Maryland.

Rouse, who scored 1,169 points and grabbed 982 rebounds during his Loyola career, had his No. 40 jersey number retired in 1993. He died May 31, 1999, in Annapolis, Md., at 56.

Loyola finished 29–2 in 1963 and led the nation in scoring. Their NCAA Tournament run included a 111–42 first-round thrashing of Tennessee Tech. That 69-point margin of victory remains an NCAA Tournament record.

The 1963 Ramblers became the first team to be inducted into the National Collegiate Basketball Hall of Fame, during 2013 ceremonies at the Midland Theatre in Kansas City, Missouri.

Jerry Lyne was an assistant coach to Ireland on that team. All-American Harkness led that team along with starters John Egan, Les Hunter, Ron Miller and Rouse, as well as reserves Dan Connaughton, Jim Reardon, Rich Rochelle and Chuck Wood. On July 11, 2013, several surviving members of the team were lauded at the White House by President Barack Obama to celebrate the 50th anniversary of the school's NCAA title. Ireland's daughter, Judy Van Dyck, and current coach Porter Moser represented Ireland at that ceremony.

Ireland also took Loyola to the NCAA Tournament in 1964, '66 and '68. Ireland retired in the middle of the 1975 season with a career record of 321–255.

Loyola remains the only Division I men's basketball team in the state of Illinois to have won the NCAA title.

While Loyola basketball players became the toast of Chicago after their 1963 championship, several of those players told me stories of their social unrest during and afterwards.

Hunter said he and his African-American teammates were made to feel unwelcome in restaurants and social establishments and on beaches on the North Side of Chicago. They spent most of their time on the South Side and in Evanston, which were more integrated.

"On campus (at Loyola)…it was almost like (white students) just stayed away," Harkness once told me. "It wasn't like a social-social thing. They just kind of stayed away so that they were not seen that much with the (black) players….It was a chill there. No one wanted to open up on campus.

"On campus, you knew your place. You didn't get into something where you thought it might be a problem. So going to a (dance) or something, you didn't do that."

And, of course, during road games, many of Loyola's African-American players were subject to a combination of ridicule and racial indignation.

"On the road, we had problems in Houston," Harkness a consensus All-American, told me. "(The fans threw coins) at us and everything. I will never forget coming through (the corridor to the locker room) and they would throw popcorn on you and things and maybe a few pennies and call out, 'Our team is red-hot, and your team is all black!'

"And then I will never forget when we went out to eat (in Houston). We sat down to eat and they said, 'No, you have to take that out.'

"I said, 'What?'

"Miller said, 'You heard the guy, let's get out of here.' He yelled at me and I was mad at Miller.

"Then when we were in New Orleans, we had to stay in separate housing," Harkness said. "(Loyola's white players) took a cab and went to the hotel.

"We had to stay with families. We had a ball because the (black) communities came out for us. We had cakes and candy and just a real nice time. Then we played Loyola of New Orleans. There were whites seated on one side of the arena and blacks on the other.

"We just went through that."

The landmark game of the 1963 Loyola season, as far as social significance, was the Midwest Regional semifinal game against Mississippi State.

The all-white Mississippi State team had been forbidden to play against racially integrated teams because of an unwritten Mississippi law.

Mississippi State players, however, were determined to compete for the national title and they decided to defy Gov.

Ross Barnett in the process. So coach Babe McCarthy and his team sneaked out of the state on a flight in the middle of the night before Barnett could have an injunction served.

Loyola won that Mideast Regional semifinal game 61–51 on March 15, 1963, at Michigan State's Jenison Fieldhouse before going on to dispatch Illinois 79–64, Duke 94–75 and defending champion Cincinnati 60–58.

Former Mississippi State center Bobby Shows told me a few years ago what that game meant to him.

"That (game) was 40 minutes that was part of my life, but the reaction of what happened after those 40 minutes is unbelievable, and it is still going on 50 years later," Shows said during a reunion of the two teams in 2012.

"The change in philosophy and the ideas, particularly in the South but also in the athletic world, has been changed for the better.

"We had two men—Dean Colvard, our president, and Babe McCarthy, our coach—who had enough guts to stand up against the status quo and the political machine of Mississippi to say, 'This is right, and these boys are going to play.'

"They are really the people who need to be honored. Us boys are just the ones who laced our tennis shoes up and played. Those two men stuck to their guns and what they believed in."

Harkness recalls that particular game with fondness as well.

"All of my life, the greatest thing that happened to me is winning the NCAA Tournament," Harkness said. "But as you get a little older, you realize that was a great feat, but it is done every year.

"But not often do you play a part of history. In 1963...a month from when Martin Luther King wrote his 'Letter from Birmingham Jail'...I mean, we were right in the middle of (civil rights history). So now the greatest game is Mississippi State-Loyola. That is the greatest thing that has happened to me."

The Ramblers had beaten an all-white Tennessee Tech team by 69 points in the first round of the tournament and found out at the last minute that Mississippi State would be their next opponent.

"There was a (temporary injunction) out for us that day to keep us from going, and we were just trying to get around it, and we did," Shows recalled. "We didn't have any pep band or cheerleaders or anybody.

"But this was an education in sportsmanship by the Loyola people...fantastic folks. They treated us with respect. There was no animosity; there were no hard plays. It was just a good ballgame. It could have been an ugly affair. They were neat guys to play against."

Hunter also remembered the clean, crisp competitiveness of that contest.

"(My teammates) all had been winners at our respective high schools, and we just felt that nobody could beat us," Hunter said. "We were aware that we didn't want a news event or any kind of fighting or anything like that. Those guys proved to be perfect gentlemen, and we didn't do anything to stir up any kind of controversy. They were a good, physical, hard team. But nothing dirty."

Leading up to that historic Mississippi State game, Harkness recalled his anxiety because of threatening correspondence he had received.

"We started getting letters from the Ku Klux Klan and other (racist individuals) at the dormitory," he said. "Letters that said, 'You better not play!' and, 'Your life is in jeopardy.' Not only me, but the other (African-American) players were getting them.

"That was on my mind, and I was a little nervous then. When all of this stuff was coming in, I realized that this was more than a game."

Hunter and Harkness said they recalled feeling the pressure from racist groups not to play in the game, as well from the black community in Chicago to win.

"All of that was coming from both sides, and we as a group—the black players, anyway—said, 'Hey, we're not going to get out of line and we are going to play for each other.' That was on our mind."

Harkness recalled the pride and commitment of all the players throughout their careers at Loyola.

"Everybody graduated," he said. "We were pretty level-headed guys. We didn't mess up. We had nine players and (eventually) 21 degrees."

Harkness still fondly remembers meeting Mississippi State captain Joe Dan Gold for the traditional midcourt handshake before the game.

"We went to shake hands after the officials gave us instructions, and I looked at him and he had like a gleam in his eyes, as if to say, 'We're here together,'" Harkness recalled.

"I really felt that. It was a warmth about him. And that is the way I looked at him…with a smile."

Harkness said it was as if the Mississippi State players were saying, "'We're here because we want to be here.' As soon as I shook (Gold's) hand, the flashes (from cameras) went off like you wouldn't believe. Then I realized this is history. This is more than a game. I could feel it."

The two schools met again on the court on Dec. 15, 2012, at Gentile Arena and the Ramblers prevailed 59–51 as the former players from both schools in 1963 looked on in the crowd of 3,321.

"That means that in 50 years of basketball, we haven't learned how to play offense yet," Mississippi State coach Rick Ray quipped.

The score was only two points off the final of that 1963 NCAA Mideast Regional tournament semifinal.

"This is a great, great feeling. And the main reason why is because (the opponent) is Mississippi State," said Harkness.

Ray became the first African-American basketball coach at Mississippi State.

"I was proud to be part of this kind of game," Moser said. "I want to give so much credit to Mississippi State and Rick Ray. I said, 'Rick, we have to play this game. This game has got to happen.'"

Ray was fired by Mississippi State following the 2015 season after going 37–60 in three years at the school.

The players in this game were born in the '90s, but tried to grasp the historical significance of its predecessor after hearing their respective coaches lecture them over the previous several months.

"A (regular-season) game like this 51 years ago wouldn't have been possible," Loyola senior Ben Averkamp said.

During a halftime ceremony, members of the '63 Loyola and Mississippi State teams were recognized.

That historic game since has been dubbed "The Game of Change" because of its impact on integration in the South, particularly in college basketball.

"I don't think anyone on our team gave any thought (in '63) to the social issues," former Mississippi State guard Larry Lee said. "We were kids. We were just gym rats who looked forward to the game."

Former Bulldogs center Shows agreed.

"We didn't know that the game was that important," Shows said. "We wanted to play in the NCAA (Tournament), and that was important. But to see the reaction of the media and others (after the '63 game against Loyola)…if this doesn't get carried down to the next generation, this historical event will be gone. We're just hoping that the younger generation will pick it up."

Jerry Harkness was the leader of the 1963 Ramblers national championship team and he displayed good sportsmanship, often under some very challenging circumstances.

Alfredrick Hughes is Loyola's all-time leading career scorer with 2,914 points. A product of Robeson High School in Chicago, Hughes was a first-round draft pick of the San Antonio Spurs in 1985.

LaRue Martin was the No. 1 pick in the NBA draft when he was selected out of Loyola by the Portland Trail Blazers in 1972. He later became a successful executive with United Parcel Service.

The 1963 Loyola basketball team defeated two-time defending national champion Cincinnati, 60–58, in overtime.

Loyola coach George Ireland offers words of advice for Johnny Egan (11) and
Ron Miller (42) during a timeout in a 1963 contest.

Al Norville (15) was a standout player for the Ramblers in the late 1950s. He later became a member of the school's board of trustees and a major donor to improve the athletic department facilities.

Johnny Egan was a starting guard on the 1963 national champions and later became a successful attorney in Chicago.

Vic Rouse gained great renown by tipping in the winning basket against Cincinnati to give Loyola a 60–58 overtime win in the 1963 NCAA championship game. Rouse later earned three master's degrees and a Ph.D.

Loyola finished 29–2 in 1963 and led the nation in scoring. Their 111–42 thrashing of Tennessee Tech remains a record for the largest margin of victory in the NCAA tournament.

An important tradition of Loyola basketball includes a team prayer before the first practice of the season.

Continued fan support for the Ramblers is a goal of coach Porter Moser. Loyola finished last in home attendance in the Missouri Valley Conference in 2017–18, despite winning the conference title.

Porter Moser was a two-year starter at Creighton and helped the Blue Jays win the Missouri Valley Conference in 1989.

Photo courtesy of Loyola Athletics

Porter Moser (right) said he learned so much about coaching and developing a winning culture from his mentor, Rick Majerus, when he was an assistant coach at St. Louis. Majerus died in 2012, but left an indelible mark on Moser, who took over the Ramblers in 2011.

Sister Jean has conducted pregame prayers with Loyola players since becoming the team's chaplain in 1994. She also has shared her version of the team's coaching strategy.

Sister Jean shows her support of Loyola players and coaches with words of encouragement, including text messages following every game, win or lose.

Sister Jean received a pair of customized sneakers from then Loyola president
Father Michael Garanzini on her 95th birthday.

Left: Original bobblehead
Below: Updated bobblehead

SISTER JEAN

Sister Jean bobbleheads were sold at a record pace following the Ramblers' trip to the Final Four in 2018.

Sister Jean celebrated her 99th birthday on August 21, 2018 with friends, students and colleagues at Loyola University.

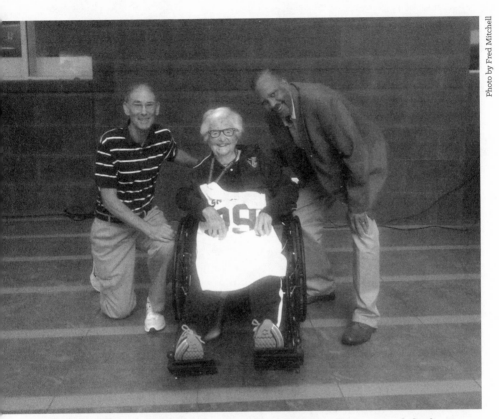

Dr. Tom Hitcho (left), Loyola's senior associate athletic director and the longest tenured employee in the athletic department, guided Sister Jean around in her wheelchair during the 2018 NCAA tournament. Sister Jean was presented a No. 99 jersey during her 99th birthday celebration on August 21, 2018.

LaRue Martin: Trying to Deal with a Tall Order

For so many years, if not decades, LaRue Martin kept his feelings bottled up.

A graceful and productive big man for the Loyola Ramblers in the late '60s and early '70s, the 6–11 center proved his mettle time and time again against the likes of Bill Walton of UCLA. He so impressed NBA scouts that he was selected No. 1 overall by the Portland Trail Blazers in 1972. He was drafted that year ahead of future Hall of Famers Julius "Dr. J" Irving and Bob McAdoo.

Indeed, Martin was one of the most celebrated and admired basketball players in Loyola's history of outstanding individual performers.

But a combination of negative factors stifled the progress of Martin on the professional level, literally leading him to drink, he says. He has been described harshly and critically over the years as being the biggest all-time bust among NBA top draft picks.

It's not as if Martin had asked or wanted to be the No. 1 overall draft pick. It was both an honor and a curse as it turned out for the affable big man.

"There was a lot of pressure. It was killing me inside," Martin says now. "You don't know how hurt I was. You just don't know. And people still talk about me behind my back. I'm 69 years old and it doesn't bother me anymore. I turned a negative into a positive. I am not doing anything wrong. I have been blessed. Say whatever you want to say about me."

But Martin, who later became successful in the business world, did not always have the benefit of perspective and maturity as lofty expectations befitting a No. 1 overall pick kept coming at him from all angles.

"Thank God I got away from that cognac. For 20-some years now I got away from that. I even joined Alcoholics Anonymous," Martin revealed. "I joined AA years ago and I had a good mentor. He passed away, but you would be surprised, because there are judges, lawyers, policemen...there are a lot of people in AA. They go by their first name only. I was shocked. I needed help, so I went for help."

Martin enjoyed tremendous success on the basketball court and in the classroom at Loyola, yet he was thrust into a very difficult position in the NBA. He soon realized his drinking was becoming a problem that affected his daily routine.

"I didn't drink with a bunch of other guys, I did it by myself," Martin said. "You know that when you do it by yourself you are in trouble. I was a heavy drinker with the cognac. Oh my God!"

After receiving professional help. Martin says he is now in control of his habits.

"I may have a little wine but nothing real heavy. I made a commitment to myself," he said.

Martin said the drinking problem came to a head one fateful night in Chicago. It was then that he realized his world was spinning out of control because of alcohol.

"I had a DUI years ago, that was 20-some years ago," he said. "I will never forget that experience. Thank God I knew some people who really pulled me through it. DUIs weren't that tough years ago. Nowadays you will lose everything.

"I could have lost my life or hit somebody. Anything could have happened. It was here in Chicago, years ago."

Not everyone with a drinking problem emerges with a happily-ever-after story. But Martin has advice for other people going through any sort of substance addiction problem.

"Seek help. And think about the Man Upstairs because He watches us. I am a Christian but I am not all that religious. But I do believe in God," he said.

As bad as his experience was with alcohol, Martin realizes his fate could have been even worse had he not exercised good judgment when it came to illegal recreational drugs.

"Thank God I never got caught up on drugs. I have gone to different places in my lifetime, and if I see drugs around, I'm gone. See you all. I am serious about that," he said.

Martin, who has carved out a very successful career with United Parcel Service, recalls how he believed that he was set up to fail in the NBA.

"When I was playing basketball, I never dreamed of being the No. 1 draft choice. They always said that I had good games against Bill Walton and Jimmy Jones, Sidney Wicks and all these guys. I did pretty well and I still hold the rebounding record at Loyola," Martin said.

"When I went to the Portland Trail Blazers...I don't want to knock anyone or say negative things, but the coach, Jack McCloskey, I guess he didn't know anything about me. And I had gotten drafted by the Dallas Chaparrals of the American Basketball Association too. My attorney told me to stick it out, but the Portland Trail Blazers had the money."

As unassuming and team-oriented as Martin was as a player, he had his spirit broken when McCloskey refused to play him when the Trail Blazers faced the Bulls at the old Chicago Stadium.

"When I was playing for Portland as a rookie, I will never forget coming here to Chicago for the first time ever to play against the Chicago Bulls. That was the most embarrassing situation of my entire life," Martin said. "I didn't get one ounce of playing time. I got tears in my eyes, I was so hurt and so embarrassed. Especially when you come back to your home town to play. I learned one thing. Connie Hawkins used to talk to me a lot, and Nate Thurmond. They said to keep your mouth shut and never say anything negative. I never said anything negative. I kept my mouth shut, took care of my family and did what I had to do."

Martin said McCloskey never took the time to explain to him why he did not get any playing time against his hometown Bulls. Not even token minutes so that he could be recognized by his hometown followers.

"If I get a little playing time, so be it. We just didn't see eye to eye," Martin said. "Now, my third year, Lenny Wilkens was a player/coach at the time. And he thought a lot about me. But that is when they drafted Bill Walton back in 1974. Bill is a great guy and he was a hell of a player. But he had health issues all the time. I played well against him in practice. But you have to get realistic playing time when you play against other opponents. I only averaged maybe five or six minutes. That was it."

Martin prides himself in keeping his cool and being a good teammate, even though the situation led to his drinking problems. He was raised to be respectful of others, especially authority figures. But the situation was eating him up inside.

"You can ask any of my old teammates, I never said anything. I just went along with everything," he said. "Because I didn't have a father then, my father was dead. I didn't want to put any pressure on my mother. She was trying to take care of my siblings, my sister and brother."

But keeping quiet did not mean he wasn't feeling the pressure to live up to the largely unattainable expectations.

Was it that pressure to succeed on the basketball court that finally got to him?

"Oh God yeah. It was a lot of pressure," he said. "Maybe some of the pressure I just couldn't handle, because when I did get a little playing time, I was trying to produce too much. I made some mistakes out there. But I will tell you one thing, the fans in Portland, Oregon treated me very well. When I got a bucket, they used to say, 'Two for LaRue.' I will never forget that."

While many of the Portland fans were patient and supportive of Martin, the local media sought to vilify the quiet top draft pick from Loyola.

"The newspapers used to beat me up a lot," he said. "*The Oregonian* used to beat me up a lot. There was a sportswriter named Wayne Thompson. He used to beat me up all the time, but he later came to me and apologized for being so critical of me. I thanked him for it. I know they have a job to do. You know how they pull that negativity out. Negativity sells. Positive things don't sell."

One particular article in *The Oregonian* described Martin as "a 6–11 emotional basket case over his own inability to prove his worth as the No. 1 college draft choice in America."

Martin averaged just 4.4 points a game with the Trail Blazers as basically a role player before being traded to Seattle.

Meanwhile, Portland would win the NBA title in 1977 with the oft-injured Walton in the middle. In previous years, Walton suffered numerous foot injuries. He also missed games after he broke his nose, wrist and leg. Walton was able to play 65 games during the 1976–77 season under new head coach Jack Ramsay.

Walton led the Trail Blazers to a sweep of the Los Angeles Lakers in the Western Conference Finals, outdueling Kareem Abdul-Jabbar. Then Walton was named Finals MVP when Portland overcame an 0–2 setback in the first two games of the series to beat the favored Philadelphia 76ers.

Martin's senior year at Loyola was spectacular and productive, even though the Ramblers finished just 8–14 on the season for coach George Ireland. Martin averaged 19.6 points and 15.7 rebounds during the 1971–72 campaign. A good free-throw shooter, especially for a big man, Martin connected on 82 percent from the line that year. Junior forward Nate Hayes chipped in with an average of 17.7 points and 6.6 rebounds. Senior guard Rich Ford was also a double-digit scorer (11.0).

And Loyola faced strong competition that season, going against Marquette, Wichita State, UCLA, Minnesota and Long Beach State. That was the year Martin outplayed Walton.

"Guys used to tell me, 'You're a nice guy but you're too soft. You need to be tougher. You can jump out of the building.' And they really pushed me to be what I am today," Martin said.

LaRue Martin: Trying to Deal with a Tall Order

In 2011, Martin appeared on *Real Sports with Bryant Gumbel* to talk about his difficult times as a pro and his bouts with drinking and depression. Martin and Gumbel had been classmates at De La Salle High School in Chicago.

When it came to picking a college, Martin told me he had many offers.

"Back in 1968, I had a number of letters coming from all different types of schools. Athletic scholarships for my athletic ability," he said. "But I decided to go to Loyola. It was a tough decision....My mother kept a shopping bag full of letters. I had about two shopping bags full. And I decided to stay here in my backyard. My mother raised us back then as a single parent, because my father passed away back in 1968 at the age of 40. And I was living in public housing. So I just wanted to stay at home. It worked out very well, building relationships, building my studies. George Ireland and Jerry Lyne, those were my two coaches back then and they treated me very, very well."

Unlike during his brief professional career, Martin felt that his coaches at Loyola cared about him as an individual and not just as a basketball commodity.

"George really concentrated, and so did Jerry Lyne, on making sure that you got good grades. Back then, if we had a couple of problems with our studies, they would make sure that we had tutors. Don't forget, I went to an all-boys private high school—De La Salle. They were tough back then. You had to study. So it was ingrained in me to study and do the best I could do. And if I had a problem with a certain subject, George and Jerry Lyne would seek out getting tutors. It worked out very well for me."

While the 1960s represented a turbulent time in our country when it came to race relations and civil unrest, the Loyola campus represented a peaceful escape for Martin.

"The support for the basketball team was great back then," he said. "The teams I was on back then, they were outstanding people and my teammates treated me very well. I had no recourse about my teammates. And we were very diverse too. I lived in Champion Hall and that was an all-men's dormitory. We had a great time. Of course, we partied. And we all studied together. And we all made a way for ourselves.

"The most important lesson I learned at Loyola was building relationships. Back then, we didn't see all of that racially divided situation that is prevalent today. We would all just hang out. It was black, white, Chinese, Hispanics. That's just the way we were. We didn't see color. Overall, we got along. We would play cards together, partied together, played basketball together."

Martin said he assimilated well on the Loyola campus and made several lifelong friends.

"And I am sad to say that a lot of the guys who were ahead of me have passed away. It's kind of scary," he said. "I am only 68. I think about the guys that I played with and I say, 'My God.' I am still blessed to be on this earth. But it is a scary situation.

"My fondest memories of my days at Loyola were the doubleheaders we used to play at the old Chicago Stadium. I got a kick out of those, and a lot of people have forgotten about those doubleheaders. You had Notre Dame coming in, UCLA, Wichita State....I played against some of the best people around.

"I was on the board of the Retired NBA Players Association (sic) and that was good camaraderie, seeing the guys. During that era, we didn't make that kind of money.

"There is life after sports. I was blessed to move on, working for Nike for a number of years and then I went on to UPS as a driver here. And I worked my way up to where I am today. My major at Loyola was sociology and my minor was education.

"I actually wanted to be a mortician years ago. The dead bodies don't bother me. But they were tough subjects at the time, so I had to change my major."

Martin's ascension in the business world was somewhat circuitous, yet steady and meaningful. He was never too proud to accept a role that was perhaps not fitting of his educational background. He tried to learn from others and he built a reputation of being a great team player, just as he had been in basketball.

"After I played professional ball I got a job with Nike. As a matter of fact, I started with the factory outlet store there in Portland," he recalled. "We started the store, and if we made money there, we used to give some of the proceeds there back to the community. I enjoyed it. Then I moved on to be a marketing shoe specialist for Nike, going to all of the high school games, marketing their basketball products. I enjoyed that job."

Martin grew as a savvy businessman while learning a lot about himself and what people skills he had to offer at each step of the way.

"Some friends of mine that I knew in Portland came to me and said, 'LaRue, have you ever thought about making a career change?' I said, 'No, not really. I am doing well with Nike.' Then they had some cutbacks (at Nike) and I decided to make a change. They said I did very well with the UPS interview process and then after about a week, they said, 'You will probably drive a Packer Car.' I said, 'What's that?' It turns out it was a truck. I started in 1987 with UPS as a driver."

Imagine seeing a 7-foot truck driver emerge from his vehicle.

"So, I did drive a truck and I finally got a uniform. But the uniform was too short. They never had such a tall, 7-foot driver before. So I had to take two pair of pants, cut the bottom off of one and sew it to the other so I could have a pair of uniform pants to fit me. I wear a size 18 boot, so what I did was take a pair of my gym shoes and dyed them black. I had my college degree and I did that job for about six months."

Just as he was ridiculed by many in the media when he failed to meet expectations as a player in Portland, Martin again found himself facing ridicule for driving a truck.

"I don't want to name names, but some people I know were laughing at me because I was driving a truck and I had been the No. 1 draft choice in the NBA. That was tough. You hear rumors about how people talk about you behind your back. They laughed at me, but see who laughs last," he said.

"After driving the truck for six months, I got promoted to be a supervisor. Then I was an area sales representative, doing a lot of their hiring for UPS. I made a lateral move to customer service, which is now called business development."

Clearly, Martin was going places in the business, and not just in a truck.

"I got promoted to Chicago by Ron Wallace. He was made the district manager and he said, 'LaRue, you are needed in Chicago. Do you want to move to Chicago?' I said, 'That's home.' I never dreamed of going to Chicago. I loved Portland. My kids were raised out there.

"So I decided to go ahead with the promotion and I went through the interview process. I did very well and got promoted to be a manager. I had a number of people reporting to me regarding the staffing in Chicago. That worked out very well. Then I was employee relations manager. And I became office manager. Then I got the opportunity to become the first community relations manager. I got another assignment of being the public affairs manager too."

Through all the personal turmoil he experienced as a professional basketball player and the alcohol addiction issues, Martin looks back at his life with deep appreciation.

"I have been blessed. Coming from where I came from, I am thankful every day," he said. "I enjoy people. That is what the corporate office tells me. They say that wherever they go, people mention my name. Which is an honor. I know people in every 50 states, plus 16 or 17 countries. And I am 7 feet tall, so I can't hide. I just try to carry myself a certain way and represent the company. Because you never know who is using your services."

And similar to all former Loyola players and alums, the Ramblers' run to the Final Four last year rekindled proud memories for Martin.

"I think it was outstanding," he said. "One thing I didn't like was when some announcers mentioned that they were a Cinderella team. I detest that phrase. They earned it. They are in the Missouri Valley Conference. That's a tough little conference. So they earned it."

And Martin, whose title now at UPS is public affairs/community services/proprietor manager, is just as proud of Loyola's reputation as a solid academic institution that cares about its athletes and their futures.

"Loyola is tied with Harvard in their graduation rate of players. That is how you sell Loyola," Martin said. "Forget about basketball, look at graduation rate. And they are doing well. Loyola is a great academic institution. Loyola has a big name."

Al Norville: A Man for All Seasons

The history and mission of Loyola University involves far more than the occasional success of its basketball program.

Established as Saint Ignatius College in 1870 by Jesuit priest and educator Father Arnold Damen, the school was renamed Loyola in 1909 and moved closer to the lakefront. The original building is now Saint Ignatius Prep.

"We are Chicago's Jesuit, Catholic University—a diverse community seeking God in all things and working to expand knowledge in the service of humanity through learning, justice and faith," the school's mission statement reads. "Loyola University Chicago is the school of choice for those who wish to seek new knowledge in the service of humanity in a world-renowned urban center as members of a diverse learning community that values freedom of inquiry, the pursuit of truth and care for others."

Loyola's promise to its students?

"Preparing people to lead extraordinary lives."

And the five characteristics of a Jesuit education have been spelled out to include:

- ▶ Commitment to excellence: Applying well-learned lessons and skills to achieve new ideas, better solutions and vital answers
- ▶ Faith in God and the religious experience: Promoting well-formed and strongly held beliefs in one's faith tradition to deepen others' relationships with God
- ▶ Service that promotes justice: Using learning and leadership in openhanded and generous ways to ensure freedom of inquiry, the pursuit of truth and care for others
- ▶ Values-based leadership: Ensuring a consistent focus on personal integrity, ethical behavior in business and in all professions and the appropriate balance between justice and fairness
- ▶ Global awareness: Demonstrating an understanding that the world's people and societies are interrelated and interdependent

Loyola's men's basketball program was established in 1913. From 1923 to 1942, the Ramblers were led by coach Leonard Sachs to a record of 223–130. The team was undefeated during the 1929–30 season before advancing to the finals of the Metropolitan Writers' tournament at Madison Square Garden in New York. Loyola finished second.

The Ramblers went to the NCAA Tournament four times between 1951 and 1975 under coach George Ireland and won the National Invitation Tournament once.

One of the best examples of a Loyola alumnus who has fulfilled this mission has been Allan Norville. He was an integral member of the basketball program and then succeeded as a businessman, enabling him to give back to his university significantly.

Norville, who has been a member of Loyola's board of trustees, was a standout player in the late 1950s for Ireland. As a senior, the 6–4 Norville averaged 11.6 points and 8.5 rebounds. That 1959–60 team included Clarence Red, who averaged 20.3 points and 16.8 rebounds. Senior Paul Sheedy averaged 18.4 points and 5.5 rebounds. Junior guard Ron Schwingen averaged 9.7 points.

Asked if he considered himself more of a rebounder than a scorer for the Ramblers, Norville quickly replied.

"I was a scorer. I broke Nick Kladis' record," said Norville, a member of Loyola's Athletics Hall of Fame. "Nick was a great guy. And rebounding...I never realized I had as many rebounds as I did. But I averaged 10 rebounds a game. I am proud of that. But I was more of a scorer when I played."

Kladis, who passed away at 81 in 2009, played at Loyola from 1949 to 1952. Kladis had starred at Tilden Tech High

School in Chicago before moving on to Loyola. He developed what he called "a crazy left-handed hook shot." He played forward, even at 6–2, and performed well enough to be drafted by the Syracuse Nationals of the NBA in 1952.

Kladis was selected to the Loyola University Athletics Hall of Fame, and he was named to the school's All-Decade team of the '50s. His No. 3 was retired after a college career that saw him score 1,046 points and gain All-America honors as a senior in 1952. He was a volunteer assistant coach on the 1963 Loyola team that won the NCAA Tournament in overtime against Cincinnati.

Kladis was among a substantial list of Loyola basketball All-Americans. The list includes: Clayton Custer (2018), Blake Schilb (2006), Alfredrick Hughes (1985), Wayne Sappleton (1982), LaRue Martin (1970, '72), Jim Tillman (1967), Jerry Harkness (1962, '63), Jack Kerris (1948), Wibs Kautz (1938, '39), Mike Novak (1938, '39), Marv Colen (1937) and Charley "Feed" Murphy (1929, '30). In 2013, Ben Averkamp was the school's first Academic All-American.

Norville was aware of the accomplishments by Kladis as he prepared to make his college decision.

"I went to Fenwick High School (in Chicago), a great school," Norville said. "I had college offers from Detroit and Loras College (in Iowa). I was really ready to go to Detroit, but we didn't have any money in the family. My brother convinced me I would be better off in Chicago because family was there."

Nearly 60 years after Norville played for Loyola, he took extreme pride in watching the 2018 Final Four appearance of his alma mater.

"That is something I am really proud of. And what was exciting last year about Loyola was that we had a real team," he said. "We didn't have these one-and-done players. Porter Moser put together a team. We didn't have that one great All-American. We had a team that played together. And if you talked to the 1963 team, that is what they emphasized more than anything. They were a team that played together. And that's what Porter had last season. The only problem in the Final Four was that the Michigan game was 12 minutes too long."

Norville has put his money where his pride is by donating millions of dollars to the university. The $26 million Norville Athletic Center opened on March 3, 2011, and the Alfie Norville Practice facility is slated to be completed in August 2019. The "Norville Challenge" was set up for donors after he put up the $1 million cornerstone gift.

"We are excited about the facility and certainly the team. They did so well. Porter Moser has done an excellent job," Norville said.

The new practice facility will be named after his late wife, who died four years ago.

"My career has been real estate and development," Norville said. "I am still very active, and I have developments here in Tucson and Alaska. And I am still working. I love what I am doing. And I just bought a hotel here in Tucson, the Double Tree Hilton. We are renovating that now. I like it a lot.

"I ended up in Tucson, Arizona. My wife had rheumatoid arthritis and the doctors told her she had to get out of Chicago and go to either Tucson or Palm Springs. So, she came out to Palm Springs and got immediate relief because it was very dry, extremely dry in the desert."

The Norvilles eventually set up business in Tucson, and he still lives and works there to this day

"She had four children and I adopted them. We lost our oldest son a number of years ago," Norville said. "I have 10 grandchildren, three great-grandchildren. I have a great family. Very proud. My grandson is in business school, my son is an attorney, my daughter is a commercial artist. Patty is in real estate here in Tucson. They are all doing well and I am very proud of them. I've got two grandsons. One at Loyola. I am so happy about that. He is in his sophomore year. His brother is a senior at Gonzaga."

Nearly 60 years since he played for the Ramblers, Norville still lives vicariously through the current team. And he loves how the overall university has evolved over the many decades.

"I am so excited about where Loyola is today. The building program and the things Father Garanzini did were brilliant," he said. "And we were kind of ahead of the curve, where a lot of universities are in trouble today. Loyola underwent a big problem 12, 13 years ago. And Garanzini came in and just turned everything around."

Norville said he is most proud that Loyola has been able to experience success in basketball without sacrificing its main mission of emphasizing academics.

"I used to tell Father Garanzini that you can have so many Pulitzer Prize winners and all kinds of awards," Norville said. "But if you have a winning basketball program and get to the Final Four and win a national championship...that will do more for your enrollment, more for the university...because you have the presence of all the newspapers and all the publicity. And the kids watch that. It's an asset to the university."

The 2017–18 Final Four season really lifted Norville's spirits.

"What Porter has done for the university is remarkable," Norville said. "He has got us back on the map and he has got the program going in the right direction. With the completion of the Alfie Norville Practice Facility, it will be terrific for all of the students, the athletic students. They now can schedule classes in a more orderly way. And they don't have to split Gentile Arena among all the different sports. So I am real happy about the addition of the practice facility and what it is going to do for the program."

Back when Norville played for Loyola, the team played its games in Alumni Gym and shared practice time in that building with a high school team.

Renowned Loyola alum Joe Gentile did the major financing for a new game arena, aptly named the Gentile Arena. But it still lacked some of the necessities for a major college program.

Nicknamed "The Baron of Barrington," Gentile was a gentle soul who was proud of his alma mater. He often said he wanted to "leave the world a better place" with his philanthropic gestures. Gentile was a very successful car dealer who also owned a suburban radio station. He passed away at 87 in 2011.

Gentile graduated from Saint Ignatius College Preparatory High School in 1942. In 1993, the Joseph J. Gentile Gymnasium was housed there. The outside of the gym includes stone artifacts from the old Chicago Stadium before it was demolished in favor of United Center.

Gentile's donations included funding scholarships and sponsoring yearly trips for 1,000 students to go to Wrigley Field for "Joe Gentile Day." He also sponsored an annual golf outing.

Gentile attended Loyola University after graduating from Saint Ignatius. He was called to active duty in 1943 during World War II, becoming a member of the V-12 Navy college officers' training program at Notre Dame and the Midshipmen's School at Columbia. Gentile was among the second and third waves of the invasion of Okinawa in World War II. He spent 20 months in the South Pacific before being injured.

Gentile returned to Loyola to complete a master's degree in psychology and then a doctorate. He became a teacher before getting into the car sales business and then owning Joe Gentile Chrysler in Barrington, Ill.

In 1994 he purchased WJJG-AM radio station and hosted a popular morning show that featured topics on sports, politics and entertainment.

Gentile was an avid Loyola basketball fan who attended most of their home games. And in 1990 he was named the Italian Sports Hall of Fame Man of the Year.

Norville picked up the baton in later years to help the university financially.

"My big effort was when they built Gentile, they didn't build enough facilities. They didn't build a weight room, they didn't build offices," Norville said. "They still used Alumni Hall for their lockers and showers. So I worked on that project for 10 years. Father Garanzini came in and I went to the development office and said we've got to do this. They were building the equipment center then and they said, 'We can't do it.' And it took me 10 years to get that done.

"Then, when they finished that, I started working on the practice facility. They had no place to practice, so they put a tremendous burden on the student-athlete. That will be resolved next August when they open the Alfie Norville Practice Facility. It is well needed, and an honor that it is going to be named after my late wife. I am really excited about that."

The Gentile Arena seats 4,486 fans. The facility also hosts the Ramblers' women's basketball team and its top-notch men's volleyball team that won a national title in 2014.

Norville has made sure that Loyola's basketball reputation has been promoted and celebrated nationwide.

"Everyone here in Tucson and a lot of people around the country know that I am a big supporter of Loyola," he said. "So last spring was a fun time for me here. I have followed the University of Arizona and I am personal friends with (Arizona) coach Sean Miller. And at the start of last season everyone's thoughts about the Final Four included Arizona. And who ends up there but Loyola. So it was exciting and fun. And it was something I have been striving to have happen for years. And it came about. Porter did an excellent job."

Looking Back: Loyola's 2017–18 Season in Review

Porter Moser talked the talk when he first arrived on the Loyola campus.

He preached the importance of creating a winning culture, recruiting players who come from winning programs, high-character individuals who refuse to take shortcuts.

During the 2017–18 season, Moser and his players walked the walk, advancing to the Final Four for the first time since 1963 and captivating a nation of both passionate and otherwise casual college basketball fans.

Minutes after the dream season ended with a loss to Michigan in the national semifinal game in San Antonio, Moser reminisced about the young men who made it all possible and the plan that remains in place.

"I just told them I remember moving them in as freshmen in the summertime into the dorm with their parents there, and they were just two high-energy, fun, young little guys," Moser told reporters.

"And it just goes so fast. And to do what they did, to win more games in a four-year span—I don't know what they won, they won 89 or some games in a four-year span. And to do it the right way. The way they are off the court. I'm telling you—I mean, not even a littering violation with these guys, dropping a Kleenex.

"These guys are just so high-character. But what they did is very hard to do. They changed—they left an impact on this school, this student body. Look at the ride the student body went on. Look at the ride the alumni went on from coast to coast.

"Look at the perception of people looking at what they did and how they did it. I mean, leaving an impact like that, they changed the perception of Loyola. And when you say that word, they impacted it.

"And they're not going to know that right now, because their pain in the locker room—I was proud of them how they held their composure here. And I wouldn't have cared if they didn't. But it was as tough a locker room as I've seen because they believed they belonged and they believed like they wanted to advance.

"And any time in life when you invest so much into something, it's hard to let it go. And those two (seniors

Donte Ingram and Ben Richardson) have invested everything. They've done everything we've asked them to do,
everything. And I'm a better person and a better coach for
coaching those guys."

Loyola's magnificent journey in 2017–18 included a Missouri Valley Conference regular-season title and an MVC
postseason tournament championship, earning the Ramblers
an automatic bid to the NCAA Tournament for the first time
in 33 years.

Moser said he thoroughly enjoyed the journey.

"This is something that's been developing over the past
couple of years, developing the culture of things. It's the little
things that separate us," he said. "We don't have to be the most
talented team, but I think we're together. But just watching
this team grow...the unselfishness of this team, the buy-in.
Ben (Richardson) talked about the attention to detail. It's a lot.

"And I've never seen—the guys are really receptive to a
competitive advantage. And they bought in. They bought in.
And I thank them for that because as coaches, the buy-in atti-
tudinally, the buy-in effort-wise...off the rails with this group.
And that's where the direction's been going. We just have
been getting better and better players and winning kids."

Moser's continued commitment to satisfying the Loyola
fan base, as well as school President Jo Ann Rooney and athletic director Steve Watson, has been relentless.

"Like I told these (players), I said we're going to be connected for life," Moser said. "I tell them in the recruiting

process, 'You're not making a four-year commitment at Loyola to play for us, you're making a lifetime relationship.' And that's what we have. That's what these guys have. It's a lifetime relationship....And I'm proud of that. I'm proud of that, that they used the word 'family' all the time. You hear that word all the time with this group. I love that. Means a lot to me."

With three starters returning and two lost, Moser entered the 2018–19 season with a 121–111 record at Loyola. His overall head coaching record was 226–212. Eight lettermen were lost, with seven returning.

The Ramblers were 15–3 in their MVC championship season and 32–6 overall—14–1 at home, 9–4 on the road and 9–1 at neutral sites.

Guard Ben Richardson saluted his coach when he talked to reporters after the win over Illinois State to claim the Missouri Valley tournament championship and automatic NCAA bid.

"The thing that I definitely would take away, what I saw, what my mom saw when he was recruiting me, was the energy and the passion that he has," Richardson said.

"He always says, like, he's going to bring his best every practice, every day, and that's what he does. He challenges us...because he knows we want to be the best we can be, and for that to happen, he's got to challenge us, and that's what he does. He brings it every day, and that's why we've gotten so much better, because we have an off-day in practice, he doesn't let it slide. It's not about who's right. He always says that. It's about getting it right.

"If we're having a down day, like, he's going to challenge us and make us fix it, make us get it right. That's stuff you don't take away, his energy and bringing it every day."

The Ramblers' Record 32-6 Season from Start to Finish

Loyola 84, Wright State 80
Nov. 10, 2017

The Ramblers' season opener was not a walk in the park against their former Horizon League opponent as there were nine ties in the first 20 minutes of action.

It took a true team effort for Loyola as four players finished in double figures in scoring, led by Donte Ingram's 21 points.

Gentile Arena was packed as Loyola made 75 percent of its shots in the first half while Wright State countered with 6 of 9 attempts from three-point range. Loyola led 45–41 at the half.

When Loyola appeared to be in comfortable control with an 81–72 advantage and about a minute to go, the Raiders stormed back with an 8–1 run as Mark Hughes connected on a pair of three-pointers. That made it 82–80 in favor of Loyola with just 26 seconds remaining.

Ingram made one of two from the line with 21 seconds left to make it 83–80 before Wright State's Alan Vest had the ball knocked away by Bruno Skokna with 10 seconds to go. Loyola would hold off the Raiders and escape with the season-opening win, their sixth consecutive opening win under Porter Moser.

After the game, Moser thanked the home crowd and credited the Raiders, who were led by Grant Benzinger's 16 points.

"Our crowd and our students truly made a difference tonight," Moser said. "I'm happy to get the win. You have to give Wright State credit. They didn't quit."

Moser and the Loyola fans also caught their first glimpse of freshman center Cameron Krutwig, who scored 17 points and pulled down seven rebounds in just 17 minutes. Clayton Custer scored 18 points for the home team and added three steals. Marques Townes finished in double figures with 16 points while grabbing five rebounds.

Loyola 96, Eureka 69
Nov. 12, 2017

Early season nonconference games provided an opportunity for Loyola to concentrate on its own game, emphasizing sharing the basketball and eliminating too many mental errors.

That was the case when the Ramblers hosted Division III opponent Eureka College and walked away with 26 assists while shooting 52 percent from the field (31 of 71). Loyola only turned the ball over eight times.

"I'm most pleased with how we moved and shared the ball, with 26 assists and only eight turnovers," Moser told reporters after the victory.

Eureka made 16 of 31 baskets (51.6 percent) in the first half.

"Eureka has tremendous shooters and runs its offense at a fast pace," Moser praised.

Aundre Jackson and Ben Richardson each had 14 points for Loyola, and Cameron Satterwhite contributed 12 points and six rebounds off the bench. Marques Townes also had 14 points, as well as seven rebounds and five assists.

Eureka was led by Shea Feehan with 17 points and five rebounds.

Loyola 66, UMKC 56
Nov. 16, 2017

Loyola hit the road for the first time during the 2017–18 season to face the University of Missouri-Kansas City (UMKC) at Municipal Auditorium in Kansas City and emerged with its third victory in a row.

The Ramblers fell behind 26–20 at the half, committing 10 turnovers. UMKC shot just 31 percent from the field (9 for 29) in the opening session, keeping Loyola within striking distance.

Clayton Custer, playing in front of his hometown fans, led Loyola with 20 points, including a run of 11 consecutive points in the second half. Aundre Jackson had 18 points as the Ramblers got their act together in the second half for a comeback win.

A 17–2 run by the visiting Ramblers gave Loyola a 58–46 lead. After a dismal shooting performance in the first half, Loyola connected on 61 percent (14 of 23) in the second half.

Loyola 88, Samford 67
Nov. 19, 2017

Loyola got off to its best start in seven years when the Ramblers handled Samford easily at Gentile Arena to improve to 4–0.

It was the combination of Clayton Custer and Marques Townes that got the home crowd most excited.

In precision-like form, Custer scored 18 points and dished nine assists, without a turnover in 38 minutes. Townes also had 18 points, with eight rebounds and three assists.

Freshman Lucas Williamson saw extended playing time for the first time and the 6–4 Whitney Young High School product produced 11 points and three rebounds off the bench in 30 minutes.

Moser's emphasis on unselfish teamwork was on display as nine of Loyola's 10 players scored in the convincing victory.

Christen Cunningham led Samford with 17 points and five assists.

Loyola 63, Mississippi Valley State 50
Nov. 21, 2017

Another strong team effort was needed to subdue the Delta Devils at Gentile Arena as Loyola improved to 5–0.

Donte Ingram, the 6–6 senior, had a double-double, scoring 12 points and grabbing 10 rebounds as Loyola overcame a 31–28 halftime deficit. Mississippi Valley State remained winless even though it opened the second half with a basket from Dante Scott to make it 33–28 in favor of the visitors.

But Loyola would go on a 23–6 run later to take a 54–41 lead to gain control. Clayton Custer led Loyola scorers with 13 points. Marques Townes had 11 points and five assists.

Tereke Eckwood had 15 points to pace the Delta Devils.

Loyola 102, UNCW 78
Nov. 24, 2017

The Ramblers reached the century mark for the first time this season as Aundre Jackson and Marques Townes combined for 48 points in the victory over the University of North Carolina-Wilmington (UNCW).

The Ramblers made 10 of 18 three-point attempts to dominate the game at Savannah (Ga.) Civic Center in the Savannah Invitational tournament.

Loyola showed its ability to adapt to a faster pace of play and shot 60 percent from the field (36 of 60). Loyola led 53–44 at the half as the game resembled an NBA-style scoring contest.

Loyola led by as many as 34 points in the second half (82–48) and eventually reached the 100-point mark for the first time since Nov. 13, 2016. Nine players scored at least a point for Loyola, including walk-on Nick DiNardi.

Jackson finished with a career-high 25 points, making 10 of 13 shots, including 4 of 5 from beyond the arc. Townes had 23 points, six rebounds and three assists. Donte Ingram had a well-rounded game of 14 points and nine rebounds. Clayton Custer finished in doubles figures with 13 points.

Jordon Talley led UNCW with 20 points.

Loyola 75, Kent State 60
Nov. 25, 2017

Hot shooting continued for Loyola in the Savannah Invitational as a second-half scoring spree broke open a one-point game at the half.

Leading just 31–30 at the intermission, Loyola would shoot 60 percent from the field (15 for 25) in the second half to pull away from Kent State. Loyola led by as many as 18 points in the second half, helped greatly by 6-of-10 shooting from beyond the arc.

Freshman Cameron Krutwig pulled down 11 rebounds as Loyola won its seventh game in a row. Donte Ingram scored 13 of his 18 points in the second half and added 11 rebounds.

Boise State 87, Loyola 53
Nov. 28, 2017

The Ramblers suffered their first loss of the season at Boise's Taco Bell Arena in a Mountain West/Missouri Valley Challenge Series matchup.

Boise State shot 57 percent from three-point range to put the Ramblers on their heels. In fact, the Broncos scored the first 11 points of the game to take Loyola out of its rhythm. Boise State rebuffed every comeback effort by the visitors and emerged with a commanding 41–20 halftime advantage.

Boise State led by as many as 35 points in the second half as Justinian Jessup led the home team with 20 points, making 6 of 7 from beyond the arc. The Broncos had five players score in double figures.

Loyola 85, UIC 61
Dec. 2, 2017

How would the Ramblers respond after suffering their first loss of the season?

They throttled crosstown rival University of Illinois at Chicago (UIC) with a blistering performance, leading 52–24 at the half and never looking back.

Aundre Jackson was virtually unstoppable, hitting 10 of 11 shots en route to a 23-point performance. Loyola's 29 assists on 34 made baskets once again showcased its unselfish team play.

"I am excited with how we played and how we shared the ball," Moser told reporters after the victory at Gentile Arena. "I was pleased with our focus. This was a complete bounce-back from Boise State and our guys were excited to get that taste out of their mouth."

Freshman Lucas Williamson was instrumental in getting Loyola off well in the first half. He scored 14 points in the first 12 minutes as the Ramblers took control 34–13. Loyola would lead by as many as 30 points in the first half (52–22).

Moser was able to empty his bench by the second half and 11 of the 14 players who were dressed wound up scoring. Loyola improved to 8–1 on the season, while UIC fell to 2–5.

Marcus Ottey led UIC with 16 points.

Loyola 65, Florida 59
Dec. 6, 2017

The Ramblers stunned the college basketball world by defeating the fifth-ranked Florida Gators at Exactech Arena in Gainesville, Fla.

It marked the first time Loyola had beaten a ranked team since 2009, when the Ramblers upset then 15th-ranked Butler. And it was the Ramblers' first time upsetting a Top 5 team since 1984, when they knocked off No. 4 Illinois.

"We have all the respect in the world for Florida and Coach (Mike) White," Moser told reporters after the game. "I am just so proud of my guys for the effort they put forth tonight. This is a huge win for our program and we hope this makes the fire burn brighter in our guys moving forward."

Perhaps reminiscent of the famous Michael Jordan "Flu Game," the Ramblers' Aundre Jackson responded to being sick the previous day by scoring 11 of Loyola's first 15 points against the Gators, including three three-point shots.

Loyola had a 34–31 halftime advantage, but Florida stormed back to take a 39–38 lead early in the second half. Instead of packing it in, Loyola responded with an impressive 11–4 run to move ahead 49–43.

With just 1:29 remaining, Florida pulled to within 61–59 on a layup by Chris Chiozza. But that is when the Ramblers' defense and Cameron Satterwhite came up big for Loyola, hitting 4 of 4 free-throw attempts in the final 16 seconds to close out the home team.

Yet another balanced team effort provided the recipe for success for Loyola. Jackson wound up with 23 points on 10-of-12 shooting from the field. Cameron Krutwig came up huge, especially for a freshman on the road against a powerhouse program. He scored 14 points and grabbed eight rebounds. The 6–9 center added three assists and three steals in his best game to date.

Florida had entered the game as the top-scoring team in the nation, but the Ramblers' tactical defense helped limit the Gators to just 59 points. Meanwhile, Loyola shot 52 percent from the field.

Loyola 80, Norfolk State 52
Dec. 9, 2017

There was no letdown in sight as Loyola hosted winless Norfolk State at Gentile Arena.

Coming off the bench, Bruno Skokna, a 6–4 sophomore guard, scored a career-high 18 points, and Donte Ingram had 15 points and six rebounds as the Ramblers breezed to victory.

Loyola set a single-game school record by converting on 71.4 percent of its shots from the field (25 of 35). The previous record was 68.1 percent against Northwestern on Dec. 15, 1990. Loyola improved to 10–1, its best start through 11 games since the 1965–66 season.

"I thought we played the right way and were really spacing it and making the extra pass," Moser said after the blowout win. "You worry about a trap game coming off the Florida win, but I was most pleased with how we made the extra pass."

Loyola made 9 of its first 11 shots to take charge of the game early. The Ramblers led 47–28 at the half en route to their 15th consecutive home nonconference victory. Loyola scored the first nine points of the second half as the lead ballooned to 56–28.

Loyola's starting backcourt of Clayton Custer and Ben Richardson sat out because of injuries, yet the quality depth on the roster stepped up its game. Loyola made 10 of 13 shots from three-point range (76.9 percent).

Milwaukee 73, Loyola 56
Dec. 16, 2017

As hot as the Ramblers were against Norfolk State, the shooting temperature plunged dramatically when they faced Milwaukee at the UWM Panther Arena.

Loyola suffered its second loss of the season by shooting just 38.5 percent from the field (20 of 52), including 21.1 percent from beyond the arc (4 of 19).

Meanwhile, Milwaukee led by as many as 20 points in the first half while connecting on nearly 54 percent of its attempts.

Milwaukee led 42–25 at the half. Loyola's Aundre Jackson, who entered the game shooting a sizzling 67 percent from the field, was held to 1-for-9 shooting against the Panthers. Donte Ingram had 13 points and 10 rebounds.

Missouri State 64, Loyola 59
Dec. 22, 2017

Playing with only eight healthy scholarship players, Loyola suffered its second loss in a row for the first time in the season.

Freshman center Cameron Krutwig came through with a career-high 18 points, but Loyola came up short against Missouri State in Springfield, Missouri. It was the Missouri Valley Conference opener for both teams.

Missouri State led 33–26 at the end of the first half, despite the best efforts of Krutwig. Missouri State closed out the first half with a 13–7 run, including a resounding dunk by Reggie Scurry.

With just 3:32 left in the game, Krutwig scored to pull Loyola within 57–56, but Missouri State jumped back on top with a basket from Alize Johnson.

Johnson led Missouri State with 24 points and 11 rebounds. Krutwig's breakout game also included five rebounds, two assists, two blocks and two steals to go along with his 18 points.

Loyola 66, Evansville 59
Dec. 30, 2017

It took a while for the Loyola offensive attack to get rolling, but the second half brought out the best in the Ramblers, who trailed 28–20 at the half.

Marques Townes scored 17 of his 19 points in the second half to fuel the resurgence.

"What a warrior-like effort by Marques Townes," Moser said after the victory that improved Loyola's record to 11–3 overall and 1–1 in the MVC.

"People will look at his 19 points. But I thought he set the tone with his defense. I thought he played good defense against Evansville's motion, which is very hard to guard. We played hard and kept grinding, even when our shots weren't falling in the first half."

Townes sparked a 15–7 second-half run to tie the score at 35. The game was tied 10 times, including 44–44.

The victory marked the 100th career triumph for Moser, who became only the sixth Ramblers coach to reach that milestone.

Aundre Jackson had 18 points coming off the bench, while freshman Lucas Williamson had eight points and five rebounds. Evansville got a game-high 20 points from Ryan Taylor.

Indiana State 61, Loyola 57
Jan. 3, 2018

A tough home loss to the Sycamores left Loyola under .500 in the Missouri Valley Conference at 1–2, with an overall 11–4 record.

The loss ended the Ramblers' nine-game home winning streak. Loyola fell behind by 16 points in the first half before rallying to close to within 33–25 at the intermission.

Loyola would take a 44–43 lead in the second half as Donte Ingram hit three three-pointers during a 19–10 run. The Ramblers later would take a 53–47 lead with 9:22 left in the game.

But the Sycamores went on a 14–4 run as the Ramblers turned cold from the field.

Loyola was fairly hot from long range during the game, hitting 57.1 percent (8 for 14). But not so much from inside the three-point line, where the Ramblers were just 11 of 31.

Indiana State got 16 points from Brenton Scott.

Loyola 56, Northern Iowa 50
Jan. 7, 2018

The Ramblers saved their best for last as Clayton Custer returned from an ankle injury and sparked his team to victory at McLeod Center in Cedar Rapids, Iowa.

The first-half break saw Northern Iowa leading 26–23. Neither team could get much going in the defensive struggle. But the Ramblers closed the game on a 11–2 run to improve their record to 12–4 overall and 2–2 in the MVC.

Loyola scored the first five points of the second half to take the lead on a three-pointer by Ben Richardson and a couple of free throws by Marques Townes.

Custer had a solid game, scoring 11 points and dishing four assists. Perhaps most importantly, he had no turnovers. Cameron Krutwig and Richardson each scored nine points. Donte Ingram had eight points and six rebounds.

Defensively, Loyola held UNI to 36.5 percent shooting for the game. Bennett Koch had 17 points to lead the Panthers.

Loyola 68, Illinois State 61
Jan. 10, 2018

Earning their first win at Illinois State since 1991, the Ramblers improved to 13–4 and 3–2 in the conference.

Defensively, Loyola forced 18 turnovers and that was key to the rare win at Redbird Arena.

"I am really proud of the guys and how they finished out the game," Moser said afterwards. "We beat a really good team tonight."

Illinois State fell to 9–8, 3–2 with the loss.

Loyola got 22 points from its reserves, including 11 from Bruno Skokna.

Donte Ingram scored the 1,000th point of his Loyola career. He became only the 19th player in school history to record 1,000 points and 500 rebounds.

Loyola 81, Bradley 65
Jan. 13, 2018

Continuing on a strong run, Loyola handled an impressive Bradley team at Gentile Arena.

Freshman Cameron Krutwig continued to show his maturity as he contributed season highs of 21 points and 13 rebounds. Loyola's performance was particularly impressive given that Bradley entered the game as the conference leader in field-goal percentage defense (.383).

The Ramblers responded by making 57.7 percent of their shots (30 of 52). Point guard Clayton Custer picked up two quick fouls in the first four-plus minutes, yet the Ramblers' offense didn't seem to miss a beat.

"I was pleased with how we answered Bradley's runs," Moser told reporters. "Custer got two quick fouls and there was no panic in us. We've got strength in numbers. Cam Krutwig just gets better and better and had really good energy and got great position tonight."

Loyola led 39–24 at the half, thanks in large part to a 15–2 run that included 10 consecutive points.

Krutwig's double-double included 10-of-15 shooting from the field. He also added two assists and two blocked shots.

Loyola 79, Southern Illinois 65
Jan. 17, 2018

The Ramblers continued to make themselves right at home with a convincing Missouri Valley win over the Salukis.

Donte Ingram (25 points) and Cameron Krutwig (18) led the way to the Ramblers' fourth win in a row.

"Southern Illinois is one of the most physical teams we have played all year," Moser said. "They don't quit. I am proud of our guys to grind it out in a tough, physical game."

Loyola overcame 11 first-half turnovers to emerge victorious. Sean Lloyd led SIU with 21 points.

Ingram's scoring performance was enhanced by his seven rebounds, three steals, an assist and a blocked shot.

Loyola 70, Valparaiso 54
Jan. 21, 2018

The fifth consecutive win for Loyola moved the Ramblers into a first-place tie with Drake in the Missouri Valley Conference.

After falling behind 27–23 at the half at Athletics-Recreation Center in Valparaiso, Indiana, the Ramblers fought back as Clayton Custer scored 15 of his game-high 18 points in the second session.

"I'm proud of our guys to come into a tough place to play and get a win," Moser said. "Clayton was phenomenal today. We turned the ball over too many times against Southern Illinois, and today had 16 assists and only eight turnovers."

A 16–1 run in the second half sealed the deal for the visitors. Loyola shot 59 percent (16 for 27) in the second half.

Custer's overall stellar performance included two rebounds, five assists and four steals to go with his 18 points. And, oh yes, he did not commit a turnover.

Bakari Evelyn led Valpo with 19 points.

Loyola 80, Drake 57
Jan. 24, 2018

A conference showdown in Des Moines, Iowa, saw Loyola mount a second-half blitz to win its sixth in a row to improve to 17–4 and 7–2 in the MVC.

Drake led 31–29 at the half before Loyola answered with a 51–26 scoring advantage in the second session.

Loyola scored 12 unanswered points in the second half to break a tie and cruise to victory at Knapp Center. Drake had fought back to tie the game at 51 on a three-pointer by Nick McGlynn.

"We've got tough kids," Moser noted. "There was no panic when Drake made that run. We trust each other and kept grinding. Our guys just warriored up."

Marques Townes scored 15 of his 17 points in the second half. Significantly, Loyola had 21 assists and just six turnovers.

Loyola's balanced scoring attack featured Custer with 14 points, Cameron Krutwig with 12 and Lucas Williamson with 10.

Graham Woodward had 14 points for Drake.

Loyola 70, Northern Iowa 47
Jan. 28, 2018

A conference rematch with the Panthers saw Loyola dominate from start to finish at Gentile Arena.

The Ramblers won their seventh in a row as Clayton Custer recorded a season-high 21 points. After leading 26–19 at the half, Loyola shot 58 percent from the field in the second half to pull away and take a two-game lead in the MVC standings.

"We knew this would be a tough, physical game, and I loved how we settled down after the first few minutes," Moser said afterwards. "Earlier in the year, if we weren't hitting shots, we let our offense dictate our defense. I thought it was a great sign of maturity that we didn't let our offensive struggles early on affect our effort on defense."

The victory matched Loyola's win total for all of the previous season. Cameron Krutwig scored in double figures (14) for the fifth game in a row.

Bradley 69, Loyola 67
Jan. 31, 2018

The Ramblers' seven-game winning streak came to a halt at Carver Arena in Peoria, Ill.

Loyola had fought back from an 11-point deficit to tie the game at 64. But Bradley got a pair of free throws from Darrell Brown with 46 seconds left and held on for the win.

"Bradley played hard and super physical and shared the ball really well tonight," Moser said. "I was proud of how we turned it in the second half and had a chance to win when we didn't play our best. And that's a good sign. You're going to have games like this in the league, and the key is how you bounce back."

Bradley led 37–29 at the half, including a 15–4 run. Loyola committed seven turnovers in the first 12 minutes.

Clayton Custer scored a career-high 23 points. Cameron Krutwig had 13 points and eight rebounds.

Loyola fell to 18–5 overall, 8–3 in the MVC.

Loyola 97, Missouri State 75
Feb. 3, 2018

Returning to Gentile Arena proved beneficial to the Ramblers as six players scored in double figures against the preseason pick to win the Missouri Valley Conference.

"First of all, I want to thank the crowd. We've been striving for an atmosphere like that," Moser said of his team's home supporters.

For the third game in a row, Clayton Custer surpassed 20 points, finishing with 23. He shot the lights out, hitting 9 of 11 from the field. Marques Townes (14 points), Cameron Krutwig (13), Aundre Jackson (12) and Ben Richardson (11) also finished in double figures in the balanced attack.

Loyola shot an astounding 61 percent from the field (39 for 64).

Loyola 72, Drake 57
Feb. 7, 2018

Yet another comfortable victory for Loyola came at the expense of Drake at Gentile Arena as the Ramblers won their 20th game.

Leading by just four points, 32–28, at the half, the Ramblers saw Clayton Custer and Cameron Krutwig combine for 22 second-half points to seal the deal.

"I thought we picked up the tempo and took care of the ball much better in the second half," Moser said. "Drake is a hard team to guard. I was pleased with how we kept at it, and in the end were able to pull away."

Cameron Krutwig led the way for Loyola with 17 points and nine rebounds. Clayton Custer had 14 points, four rebounds, four assists and three steals.

Overall, Loyola had 21 assists and just nine turnovers.

Loyola 75, Indiana State 71
Feb. 10, 2018

Loyola maintained its two-game lead in the Missouri Valley Conference with the victory over the Sycamores.

"This was a grit game on both ends," Moser said. "Every time (Jordan) Barnes and (Brenton) Scott shoot, you think it's going in. But I was really pleased that we made some plays down the stretch."

Loyola trailed 36–31 at the half at Hulman Center in Terre Haute, Ind. Loyola had taken an early 16–9 lead before Indiana State made 9 of its final 16 shots in the half.

Donte Ingram led five Ramblers in double figures with 17 points. Loyola shot 64 percent from the field in the second half.

Indiana State got 17 points from Barnes.

Loyola 80, Valparaiso 71
Feb. 14, 2018

The Crusaders gave the Ramblers just about all they could handle in a hard-fought conference game at Gentile Arena.

Valparaiso missed its first seven shots as the Ramblers' defense dug in. But the visitors fought back to keep the pressure on the home team.

"I'm really proud of our guys. Valpo gave us everything and more tonight," Moser praised. "Donte Ingram really stepped up in the second half. And Clay (Custer) was efficient, with 20 points on 11 shots."

In the end it was the Ramblers' efficiency that prevailed. They shot nearly 61 percent from the field and turned the ball over just six times.

The 18 points gave Cameron Krutwig 10 consecutive games in double figures, and he added seven rebounds.

Loyola 76, Evansville 66
Feb. 18, 2018

At least a share of the Missouri Valley Conference title was clinched by Loyola with its 10-point win over the Purple Aces at Ford Center in Evansville, Indiana.

It marked Loyola's first conference championship since 1984–85, when it captured the Midwestern Collegiate Conference title before advancing to the NCAA Tournament Sweet 16.

"We've got more work to do, but I am so proud of our guys to come in here and get a tough road win," Moser said. "Turnovers really bothered us today, but Donte Ingram stepped up and hit some big shots and we made a lot of intangible plays that you need to have in order to win championships."

Ingram connected on a clutch three-pointer after Evansville had pulled to within three in the second half. Ingram's trey made it 63–57 in favor of Loyola.

As usual, it seemed, the Ramblers saved their best for the second half. They shot 70 percent (14 of 20) in the half after trailing 28–27 at the intermission.

Loyola 75, Southern Illinois 56
Feb. 21, 2018

An outright Missouri Valley Conference title was at stake for Loyola and the Ramblers took full advantage.

Loyola hit eight of its first 10 shots and spurted to a 21–8 lead in the first six minutes. The Ramblers led 44–36 at the half.

"These kids are winners and are a special group," Moser said. "They were so focused. I think a key was how we started the second half because SIU finished with a nice run to finish the first half."

The second half started favorably for the Ramblers, however, as they outscored SIU 12–3 over the first four minutes.

Clayton Custer again led a balanced Loyola scoring attack with 16 points (24–5, 14–3). Loyola shot 57.4 percent from the field for the game after entering as the No. 2 team in the nation in field-goal percentage.

Loyola 68, Illinois State 61
Feb. 24, 2018

A capacity crowd of 4,963 fans cheered on the Ramblers at Gentile Arena as Loyola won its 25th regular-season game, the most victories since the 1984–85 season.

"What a great atmosphere and a great college basketball game that was," Moser said. "I'm really proud of my guys."

A poignant pregame ceremony saluted the seniors on the Loyola roster who were playing their last game at home. At the end of the game, the Ramblers celebrated by cutting down the nets and hoisting the Missouri Valley Conference regular-season trophy.

The 15 conference victories were a Loyola school record.

Missouri Valley Conference Tournament, St. Louis, Missouri

Loyola 54, Northern Iowa 50
March 2, 2018

The top-seeded Ramblers had to scramble a bit in the first round of the Missouri Valley Conference tournament against the Panthers yet prevailed by virtue of a 14–2 run in the second half.

UNI (16–16) was the ninth seed in the tournament, held at the Scottrade Center in St. Louis. Loyola remained on a roll by winning its eighth consecutive game to head into the MVC semifinal round.

"I thought it was a classic Valley game, especially with Northern Iowa," Moser said. "It was gritty. It was tough. It was ugly at times. Just crazy how well they defend you. I was proud of our guys' mentality. There was no panic."

Reminiscent of many of their previous games, the Ramblers started out slowly on offense, converting only one of their first 10 shots. But their intrepid defense kept them in the game. By halftime, Loyola had taken a 25–21 lead into the locker room.

"I think there was more panic in our fans than there was in our guys," Moser said of the slow start. "You could just feel them pulling their hair out. And these guys, we were like, hey, we got to keep guarding....Both these guys (Ben Richardson and Marques Townes) made some big plays and some big defensive plays. We came out of a timeout when we really needed an intangible lift, and Ben got that steal in the corner. That's why he's Defensive Player of the Year.

"Marques was really getting downhill, and (it was) just a classic gritty game."

After the score seesawed a bit, Loyola put together a 14–2 run that included a long three-pointer by Richardson. Townes wound up with 13 points and eight rebounds. Donte Ingram also scored 13.

Richardson checked all the boxes as he was credited with nine points, six assists, four steals, a block and a rebound.

"I think it was the flow of the game," Richardson said of his second-half performance. "I mean, Northern Iowa is super tough defensively. They're going to make it tough on you the whole game. You're not going to get a whole lot of looks.

"We want to get a lot of possessions, and they kind of slowed us down a little bit. I didn't feel like I had a lot of looks in the first half, and then I kind of just let it come to me, tried to be aggressive, tried to make plays. Trying to get downhill most of the second half, I think, would be more of what I was focusing on, and then some good things happened."

Panthers forward Bennett Koch said he expected a second-half run from the Ramblers.

"They're a great team. We knew they weren't going to make it easy for us," said Koch. "I think it was a little of them being a good team locking it down and playing good defense, and then us just having a bad roll."

Northern Iowa head coach Ben Jacobson marveled at Loyola's precision offense.

"That was good basketball game. I expected that it was going to be hard-fought, and it was," Jacobson said. "I thought the guys did a good job of defending on a lot of possessions. They're just a hard team to stay in front of. They've got such a high skill level that you just feel like you're constantly turning circles and constantly chasing them. They had us in that mode, some in transition, some in half-court….That's not different than what they've done all year, but that makes it difficult."

Loyola 62, Bradley 54
March 3, 2018

Loyola had a bit easier time, dispatching the Braves in the MVC Championship semifinal game.

The Ramblers led by as many as 14 in the first half before settling on a 36–25 advantage at the intermission.

"I love our guys' mentality. They just refused to quit," Moser said afterwards. "You look at how many grind-out games we've had, especially in the last several weeks. And we just find ways to win. Different guys, different nights. That is what it is special about this group."

Loyola's signature defense forced 11 first-half turnovers by Bradley. In the second half, Bradley mounted a resurgence to pull to within 47–45. And then once again at 54–53 with 6:42 left to play. But down the stretch, Loyola's defense tightened up again and held the Braves without a field goal in the waning minutes.

Bradley was held to 40.9 percent shooting by Loyola for the game. Clayton Custer and Marques Townes each scored 12 points for the winners.

Loyola 65, Illinois State 49
March 4, 2018

Familiar rivals met for the Missouri Valley Conference tournament championship game as Loyola finished off Illinois State.

Most significantly, the win gave the Ramblers an automatic bid to the NCAA Tournament. Their 10th consecutive victory put them in the Big Dance for the first time in 33 years.

"I've said the words 'God has a plan' about a million times the last 10 years," Moser said after the win. "But I'm blessed to coach this group. It's a special group of how much they invested, and they did it the right way."

Ben Richardson tried to let the reality set in that Loyola was now heading to the NCAA Tournament for the first time in 33 years.

"This is what we've been dreaming about. This is what we've been talking about," Richardson said. "We knew we had a lot of potential, a lot of pieces this year. We knew that it was going to take defense.

"Tonight, I think they said we finished—that we let up (30) percent from the field. That was something we talked about early this year going into the preseason, how are we going to be different from last year? We had a good offense last year, but we needed to be able to get stops and be a top defensive team to win a championship.

"To go from there and everyone have a buy-in and improve in that aspect, it's crazy. It's so special. We have such a special group of guys. We're so close. I wouldn't want to share this with anybody else."

This time the Ramblers got off to a great start to lead 9–2 while their defense helped force the Redbirds to miss nine of their first 11 shots. It was 36–27 at the half, with Loyola on top.

With 4:17 left in the game, Loyola led by 20 points (62–42) and Rambler fans began sensing the start of a dream situation. Donte Ingram finished with 18 points and eight rebounds. Meanwhile, Loyola's team defense limited ISU to 30.1 percent shooting from the field (21 for 66).

Ingram sounded more excited about his team's overall defense than his offensive numbers.

"Coach has been preaching, since I stepped foot on campus in that locker room, the top three teams in defense in the conference are always the top three teams in the conference," Ingram said. "That was our focus, defense. That's what wins championships. And we've tried to do a great job with that all year. That's how we got a lot of wins."

Clayton Custer and Marques Townes were asked if they ever could have imagined going to the NCAA Tournament when they first decided to transfer to Loyola.

"I just felt like this would be a special group," said Townes, who transferred from Farleigh Dickinson. "I knew that guys wanted to get to the NCAA Tournament last year, but it didn't happen. They fell short. I told Coach I was going to do everything I can to try to get these guys back there.

"I'm just so proud of these guys. We worked so hard in the summertime. We pushed everything together, and I just love these guys so much."

"Yeah, it's obviously a scary thing to transfer, it's a super scary situation," Custer said. "It's a low point because there's so much unknown. I feel like I couldn't have come to a place that would have welcomed me more than they did here. I mean, they welcomed us in with open arms; the whole coaching staff is there for us. I mean, even more so—like even off-the-court stuff with school, I feel like I can text them about anything in my life or anything.

"I just remember just seeing Coach's passion and, like, you can just see it in his eyes how much he cares about this. And it's amazing to see that every single day. There's not one day that he doesn't show up.

"And I just believe in him. I believe in everything he was doing. Obviously, Ben had a big part in it too, just because I grew up with him and that was a comfort level there. But just…I 100 percent believed we could get to this point when I decided to come here. I'm just so happy that it's gotten to this point."

Winning the MVC title in St. Louis took on even greater personal significance for Moser, who was an assistant coach to Rick Majerus with the St. Louis Billikens. Majerus, who led

Utah to the Final Four in 1998, died in 2012 at 64 after years of heart issues.

"He would want to know if I was coming home tonight so we could go to The Hill and eat dinner," Moser said with a pleasant smile. "He obviously had such a huge impact on my life. He reinforced how to do things the right way. He was—you know, he was so much about doing it the right way with good kids.

"As you can see in the last 15 minutes, just listening to how these kids speak to each other, how well-spoken they are, how they care about each other. They're just a high-character group.

"That means a lot to me to do this the right way, and that's what he'd say to me. He goes, 'You know, these kids play smart and tough.' He'd love that. But very, very blessed. I've thought about him a lot while I'm here."

Moser also took time to appreciate realizing a seemingly distant dream to take the Ramblers to the NCAA Tournament.

"You know, I think it means a ton. I remember getting the job, and I was telling friends and family—like, I'm a Catholic kid from Chicago—'How cool would it be for Loyola to go to the NCAA Tournament?'" Moser said.

"And some of them were looking at me like I was nuts. Just, it means a lot. To see the amount of students that made the trip, to see us—you want that in a college. I kept on talking to the students when I go to all these speaking things with the students. I'm like, 'You want this as a part of your experience.'

And I just hope that it starts the trajectory of traditions and cultures where there's so much spirit.

"There was so much Loyola spirit here this weekend in St. Louis, more than I've ever seen. And that is just hopefully the beginning, and I think, when you have a watershed team like that, a watershed moment, being this weekend and this season, you hope it goes in a direction of—that it changes. And these guys, I believe, have made an impact on this university that will last, hopefully forever. But I hope people look at Chicagoans with that kind of enthusiasm, or Loyola of Chicago with that kind of enthusiasm and passion."

NCAA Tournament, Dallas, Texas

Loyola 64, Miami 62
March 15, 2018

Donte Ingram's clutch three-point shot with 0.3 seconds remaining will go down in history as one of the most impactful plays in Loyola athletic history.

It gave the 11th-seeded Ramblers a two-point win over the sixth-seeded Hurricanes and injected even more confidence into a team that felt "Why not us?"

Fans were stunned at American Airlines Arena in Dallas, as were fans watching across the nation, even if their tournament brackets had been "busted" by the Ramblers.

The victory was the 11th in a row by the red-hot Ramblers.

Following the miraculous win, Moser, Townes, Custer and Ingram met the media to try to explain what had just happened.

"With these young guys...we're in the huddle. Even when we were down seven, it was just about keep fighting, keep fighting," Moser said. "There's no quit in these guys. They believe. They share the ball. We had 19 assists. And a great example is that last pass to Donte with Marques to find it. They made big shots. Clay made a big shot on an action we run in the corner. Very, very blessed that we have kids that do not quit, that are resilient."

Ingram tried to describe the shot and the feeling he had when it went in.

"I mean, it was a great feeling," Ingram said with a huge smile. "I thank Marques for making that pass. Any one of us could have hit that shot, but I was just fortunate enough to be in the position. And when I seen the shot and I had space, I was confident, and it went in, luckily."

Ingram was asked about the plan laid out before the big three-pointer.

"Well, if our (big) man would have got the rebound, we would have called a timeout. Since a guard got it, you know, Coach just had faith in us and said, 'Let's go. We're under attack.' At that point, it is just up to us to make a play, and luckily, we came through with a play," Ingram replied.

With about a minute to play, Custer made a three-point shot to tie the game at 60 before Miami called a timeout.

"I mean, that's another example of Ben knowing where I'm going to be before anybody else knows where I'm going to be," Custer told reporters. "No, it's a credit to Coach. I mean, we work on situations like that in the last four minutes every day in practice.

"We try to be the best team at executing down the stretch. And I mean, we've worked on that action a hundred times. We felt comfortable running it, and we executed it perfectly. And I was lucky enough to make the shot."

The players were asked how they were able to show such composure in that stressful situation.

"We talk about that in the huddle the last four minutes. Just give it everything you've got and don't break, don't break on defense, just stay and execute our plays," Townes said.

"We just talk about just never give up. And (Moser) just talked about that in the huddle, Coach always emphasizes, 'Don't break, don't break. These last four minutes, don't break.'"

Custer explained it this way:

"Coach does a great job of making sure we keep our blinders on. In a situation like the NCAA Tournament, there's so many distractions around us and cameras following us around everywhere.

"He closed the doors on everybody and just told us, like, it's time to play, it's time to focus. And I don't feel like we had pressure on us to win. I mean, we're in the situation where we can go out there and play free and play the way we've been playing all year. And I think we're a scary team if we're playing free and like we have nothing to lose. I think that's a big part of what we've been doing."

The players also talked about the thrill of seeing the reaction of Sister Jean following the dramatic first-round win.

"Sister Jean, she has meant so much to me personally and obviously the team," Ingram said.

"She is there before every game. She's saying a prayer before every game. After the game, she sends a general email to the team. And then at the end of the email, it'll be individualized. 'Hey, Donte, you did this, you rebounded well tonight.

Even though they were out there to get you, you still came through for the team.'

"She's just so special, her spirit. She's just so bright, and she means so much to the city of Chicago and Loyola, obviously, and the team."

Townes said he considered Sister Jean to be sort of a de facto coach.

"Yeah, she gives us great, great scouting reports," Townes said. "Sister Jean, she's just a wonderful person. Just to have her around and her presence and her aura, when you see her, it's just like the world is just great because just her spirit and her faith in us and Loyola basketball and just her being around. She's the biggest Loyola fan I've ever met in my entire life. And just having her and her giving us our pregame prayers, just having her here is just a real blessing."

Custer said he also feels very comforted by Sister Jean.

"Sister Jean is, like, when you talk to her, when she's in the same room as you, it warms your heart," Custer said. "She just has such a positive energy around her. I mean, she's obviously just amazing. For her to be doing what she's doing at her age, it's amazing, and it's inspiring, and I think—I mean, I think her prayers definitely mean a little bit extra when she prays for us. She's huge for us, and she's huge for our success."

While Ingram received due praise for his game-winning shot, it was the Loyola defense that made that play possible. And defense was the trademark of the 2017–18 team.

"I would say defense is at the top, the top, top, top with us because defense wins championships," Townes said. "I mean, offense can win us a couple games here and there, but we really take pride in our defense. You know, we set game goals for our defense. We want to keep them at a certain percentage, limit them to a certain amount of offensive rebounds on the glass. And you know, I don't think we got our field-goal percentage today, but that just shows that we don't ever quit. I've never seen these guys quit all year, and we're just looking forward to this next game."

Minutes after hitting the winning shot against Miami, Ingram was asked if it had all soaked in yet.

"As a kid, this is what you grow up seeing, hoping that you can be in that moment," Ingram told reporters. "For me to be in this position with these guys, with this coaching staff, I wouldn't want it any other way, and I'm just obviously blessed to hit that shot, and I'm happy that we can get on and advance to Tennessee."

Moser, who is generally upbeat and positive, was asked if he ever doubted his team's ability to come back against Miami.

"The only negative sign I saw was the first couple minutes defensively in the second half. And then we had a media (timeout), and we kind of got after them a little bit, and then we were guarding the way we were guarding," Moser said.

"But, like, we were down seven at a timeout. I think I called a timeout, and it was all about us regrouping, moving forward. We'd been in that position many times where we've gotten down, and we don't quit.

"These guys understand that there's a lot of possessions left. They understand that we can have great possessions on both ends. And that's what it was about. It was about great possessions, getting the defense—and we always talk about this, and I think you've heard me say this, our defense has got to dictate our offense.

"I think we came out of that timeout, and then Ben Richardson got a great steal and then kicked it up, and we got a layup. That's one of those intangible plays we talk about. Our defense created it. We needed a play like that bad.

"It shows you the intangibles with Ben. You look at Ben, Ben didn't score tonight, (but) he was unbelievable. He had some really good plays defensively, and he had eight assists, one turnover, one block. I mean, that's got to be a career (best). One steal, five rebounds. I mean, the kid does anything he needs to do to win, and he is just a winner.

"It was about getting back, grinding defense, sharing the ball."

Loyola 63, Tennessee 62
March 17, 2018

Loyola's one-point second-round victory over Tennessee was no less dramatic than its upset of Miami in the first round.

This time it was Clayton Custer hitting the game-winner with 3.6 seconds left. It didn't exactly go "swish." It was more like "clank, clank, swish."

This time it was the third-seeded Volunteers (26–9) who fell victim to the Ramblers in Dallas. The victory thrust Loyola into the Sweet 16 for the first time since 1984–85.

"I mean, Coach put me in a position to make a play at the end, and I'm very appreciative of that," Custer said afterwards. "I mean, the only thing I can say is, 'Glory to God for that one.' I mean, the ball bounced up on the rim, and I got a good bounce like that. But the only thing I could think about after the game is that that's all the hard work...that you put in to get in a situation like this, and all those hours, those waking up early in the morning and working out. For all that hard work to come up to that lucky bounce is worth it, and I think all the hard work, the basketball gods helped that one go in, and I'm just super blessed to be in this situation right now."

Loyola led 29–25 at the half, but there was a sense that Tennessee might wake up and make a serious run. But it was Loyola that came out of the locker room on fire as Custer and Ingram hit back-to-back three-pointers to make the score 38–29. Lamonte Turner hit a three for Tennessee, but Lucas Williamson responded with a trey for the Ramblers.

When Loyola went up 50–41, the Vols called a timeout.

"I mean, it's amazing what you can do when you get a group of people believing and that are really tight," Moser said of his squad. "I've said that since day one. I've said it for years now. The guys—we have a close-knit culture, and the guys in the locker room pull for each other. They share the ball. It's just amazing. They really—we all, we really believe."

Loyola took a double-digit lead at 58–48 when Ben Richardson found Aundre Jackson with a pass for an uncontested layup.

Tennessee then roared back with a 14–3 run to take the lead 62–61 with 20 seconds left. Custer then provided the tantalizing jumper that landed for a Loyola victory.

Loyola had called a timeout with 10 seconds left to set up the final play.

"I was going to kind of dribble over to the left," said Custer, who finished with 10 points. "And then Krutwig was going to come up and act like he was going to set a screen and then drop it. And kind of just let me go with my right hand...and I got a good bounce."

Ben Richardson was asked how it felt to see his best friend since childhood make that game-winning shot.

"I've seen him make one, two dribbles, one-two pull-up probably a million times," Richardson said. "And I have so much faith in that shot just because I've seen him make it— like when we're just working out and stuff, he makes it, like, a 98 percent clip.

"So before games, I'm always just, like, get to that one-two pull-up, get to that one-two pull-up. We try to tell him because it is such a high-percentage shot for him. He knocks it down so much. It is fitting that he hits a big shot going one-two pull-up like we've been doing in the gym for our whole lives working on that shot. I'm so happy for him in this moment. It's something I'll never forget."

As Loyola prepared to enter the Sweet 16 at Philips Arena in Atlanta, Moser was asked to reflect on the state of Loyola's program from the time he took over seven years ago.

"It was tough. It was tough," he began. "I mean, it's been a grassroots rebuild. Everything from a couple hundred people at games to during games you could walk through—I remember my family members said they would walk through the student union, and there were more people in the student union than in the arena.

"It was at the bottom of the Horizon League, which is a good league, and then we moved to the Missouri Valley, and it just—it's been a grassroots rebuild. And I'm blessed, so blessed that Loyola University, the administrators, the fan bases, they were steadfast on how I was saying I was going to do it with good kids, good people. We weren't going to bend on the academic reputation.

"All our kids graduate. We've got high-character kids, and it was a credit to them. And in this day and age—because I know fan bases all over want it so fast, they want it so fast. And it's hard. It's hard to have a rebuild because you've got to get your kids in there that you recruit. And you're not going to hit on the first recruiting class. Everyone was like, 'Well, the second year they'd better win.' Well, the first recruiting class is freshmen.

"So it takes time to get those kids where your recruiting class comes in, and the older kids are, like, 'This is how our culture is.' And I'm blessed that the university had the same vision, and this is the vision. I said it so many different places I spoke. I go, 'Can you imagine getting to the NCAA Tournament, advancing? Can you imagine our university, Chicago?' And I'm from the Chicago area, and I just kept on pounding that vision.

"And I've had a great coaching staff. My coaching staff is an extension of everything we're doing, and it isn't just one person. It isn't just me. It is an absolute wide stretch of people at Loyola that has had that vision to do it the right way with a good foundation of great kids, great student-athletes."

NCAA Tournament Sweet 16 and Elite Eight, Atlanta, Georgia

Loyola 69, Nevada 68
March 22, 2018

Yet another heart-stopping game awaited the Ramblers as they held off Nevada in the South Region semifinal at Philips Arena in Atlanta.

Loyola advanced to the Elite Eight for the first time since the 1962–63 season when it won the NCAA title.

Loyola led 28–24 at the half while holding Nevada without a point for the final 7 minutes and 55 seconds of the session. Loyola took a 36–24 lead early in the second half as Townes and Richardson scored four points each.

Minutes later, Custer hit a jumper to give Loyola a 40–28 advantage. The Ramblers connected on 75 percent of their second-half shots (18 for 24) to keep the heat on the Wolf Pack.

Among the distractions for Loyola during the days leading up to the Nevada contest was getting to the arena for practice. The expected police escort to the facility never arrived and the bus driver didn't know where the arena was.

"Our guys handled it a lot better than me," Moser said. "I guess my immaturity came out. But no, it was frustrating. We couldn't get here. But when we got here, everybody was great.

"We had a good practice. Guys got a lot of shots in. We went over a lot of things. You know, you can either let it bother you or not, so we're not going to let it bother us, and everything since that moment has been great. People here have been great, and we've been able to—hey, maybe it's a first—fight adversity. You're going to have to do that in this situation."

Indeed, the Ramblers did against Nevada.

Donte Ingram and Custer hit shots to give Loyola a 48–38 lead with just over 13 minutes left to play.

"The first time I interacted with Donte was over at Simeon High School doing a recruiting visit and watching him come from a great program where the kids are about winning," Moser reflected. "Their coach is a terrific coach, getting after the guys in terms of discipline and playing the right way. And I just saw (Donte's) athletic ability first, and then I saw his skill. And I like to mismatch guys."

After Nevada tied the game at 59 with four minutes left, Aundre Jackson hit a big three-pointer for Loyola. After Nevada pulled to within 66–65, Townes hit a three-pointer as the shot clock expired to make it 69–65 with just seven seconds left.

"I'll probably remember it for the rest of my life," Townes said. "I mean, it really doesn't get any better than that."

Moser said, "He was a warrior."

Four members from Loyola's 1963 championship team were spotted courtside during the game: Captain Jerry Harkness, John Egan, Rich Rochelle and Les Hunter.

"I love that Loyola Nation, Rambler fans all over the country, because pride is an awesome human trait," Moser said. "And to see the pride in Loyola alumni, fans and Chicago is something that is great."

Loyola 78, Kansas State 62
March 24, 2018

Loyola struck quickly against K-State, taking a 15–5 lead before emerging with a commanding 36–24 advantage at the intermission in the South Region final at Philips Arena.

The convincing victory vaulted the Ramblers to their first Final Four since 1963.

Ben Richardson scored a career-high 23 points, including six three-pointers.

"I got a good look to start the game, and that kind of started me off. And then I hit a contested one, and then after that I was really in a rhythm. The rim starts to look a little bit bigger," Richardson said.

"I've got to credit my teammates for finding me. That's what's so special about our team. We've got so many unselfish guys, and we have so many weapons. And like we've been saying, it can be anybody's night. We've shown that so far this tournament. Each one of these guys has had a big night.

"I was in a rhythm and they were finding me, and so I just kept taking shots. They went down, and it was a big-time game, the biggest game of my life. So yeah, I guess I kind of just blacked out on some of those celebrations."

Loyola shot 57 percent from the field, hitting 27 of 47 attempts. Meanwhile, Kansas State converted only 35 percent (23 of 66).

"That was one of our game goals, to try to have them shoot under 40 percent for the game," said Marques Townes, who scored 13 points.

"We knew that Kansas State was a gritty team, and they'll get up on you and make you turn the ball over. But I felt like we took real care of the ball today. We were selfless today and Ben had a real good game.

"We tried to limit their offensive rebounding. We made some big-time plays and big-time shots at certain crucial moments. And like I said before, they shot (34.8) percent for the game, and I feel like us getting those stops resulted and contributed to the W."

Clayton Custer agreed that suffocating team defense was as big a key to the Ramblers' success.

"Yeah, I mean, the first thing we talk about, when we talk about any team or scouting any team, is how we're going to stop them," Custer said. "We talk about defense. Coach makes sure that we're locked in on the defensive end. Our coaching staff works harder than anybody I've ever seen to know every single tendency of every single player, and we have a specific way of how we want to guard things.

"The first focus is defense for us. Yeah, people talk about our spacing and the way we move the ball and how unselfish we are, which I think that that's expected because we do do a good job of that. But I think maybe—yeah, our defense is definitely the key to us winning these games."

Townes converted a three-point play to give Loyola a 69–52 lead that dashed any hopes of a comeback by Kansas State.

"Our defense dictates everything. We say it all the time," Moser said.

"Our defense dictates our offense. We talked a lot about the Miami game and Tennessee game; we just kind of got shell-shocked in the first four or five minutes. Then we called a timeout, and then we got settled in because I thought we were playing defense quiet. They came out really noisy on defense. They were guarding right in front of us, and normally you'll hear our bench yelling everything, and they were yelling switches, they were yelling different things. They thought they were running, and you could just see them—you could just see them getting stops and then running. You could just see the energy of creating some offense with our defense.

"I think they knew right away that our defense was dictating our offense, and just the confidence was just growing, moving and spacing the ball, because they knew they were getting stops."

NCAA Tournament Final Four, San Antonio, Texas

Michigan 69, Loyola 57
March 31, 2018

Michigan overcame a 10-point second-half deficit to end Loyola's dream season in the Final Four at the Alamodome in San Antonio.

The third-seeded Wolverines relied heavily in the second half on center Moe Wagner, who finished with 24 points and 17 rebounds.

"I had a lot of easy offensive rebounds and they just happened to occur. The second half, we ran a little more set plays just because we were in front of our bench, so it's easy to call," Wagner said.

"And our offense was a lot more organized. It just happened to be like that."

Wagner joined Larry Bird and Hakeem Olajuwon as the only players to record at least 20 points and 15 rebounds in a national NCAA semifinal game.

"Wow. If you put it like that, that's probably cool," Wagner gushed. "But to be honest, I kept looking possession by possession....We had trouble scoring the first half. We scored 22 points and that was kind of the only way we found our way to the basket, grab offensive rebounds and get second-shot opportunities.

"And honestly I just tried to do my job. The shots were falling the second half. It's a lot more fun when the ball goes to the net. And yeah, it just worked out that way."

Turnovers exacerbated the problem for the usually efficient Loyola team, which committed 17 during the game. The 17 turnovers led to 22 Michigan points.

Loyola led 29–22 at the half and 32–22 early in the second half before the wheels started to come off.

Michigan outrebounded Loyola 36–32, but the most startling disparity was in the turnovers. Loyola had 17 and Michigan 11. The Wolverines also had 10 steals compared to the Ramblers' five.

"I mean, obviously, you don't want to go in those droughts and give it to teams to go on runs like that," Donte Ingram said of the second-half meltdown.

"I think this team was trying to be aggressive, trying to make the right plays. I think a couple times we got a bit sped up or (had) a miscue. And it happens sometimes. But unfortunate for us, obviously, to go through that drought. But give credit to Michigan, they played a great game."

As seniors, Richardson and Ingram tried to put into words what the journey to the Final Four meant to them personally as they shared their emotions.

"Me and Ben have been in this together since day one," Ingram said. "Me and him are the only guys on the team that have seen all this come up from day one, along with Coach.... We've come a long way from freshman year to maybe 100 (fans) on a good day coming to the game to being able to buy into the culture and return things and be able to make people in the city of Chicago proud.

"So obviously, this is something that will keep us connected for the rest of our lives. I love all these guys like brothers. We're all family, the players, the coaching staff. And I won't forget this."

Richardson was quickly able to look at the big picture right after the difficult loss.

"I mean, it hurts right now, and we're disappointed. But we're going to be able to have a lot of pride in the fact that we made a name for ourselves and kind of let the whole country know what we're about and worked hard for it," he said. "And we earned everything that we got.

"And I think we did it the right way. And it's special to see kind of what stage that we were able to get to. And despite going out this way, we're going to never forget this. And I think a lot of people will remember this run for a long time."

Even Michigan coach John Beilein sang the praises of Loyola and its defensive efforts.

"We're just elated to get a win like that and the way we did it," Beilein said. "We see some really good defenses in the Big Ten, really good. I would argue it's the best defensive league in the country.

"And we saw some great defense. They're a little bit smaller at the forward positions, or at some of the positions, and they can really get in to you and guard. And they really gave us problems in the first half. They rotated so quickly. And this has been our dilemma all year long: How are people going to guard a shooting five? And we have to adjust as the game goes on. We didn't adjust very well.

"But the second half, after we saw…their actions and then we needed to make some shots, we couldn't make them for a while, but then we did. And our young guys came in there—all of a sudden we took off like crazy. Everybody is really happy, and we're ready to move on to the next game."

Loyola freshman center Cameron Krutwig scored 17 points in 24 minutes against the Wolverines. But Wagner was able to take over in the second half.

"I knew they were trying to punch us—first of all, you've got to give them a lot of credit, their set plays are incredible," Wagner said.

"Tough to guard. And their big man does an incredible job down there as a freshman.

"So we had to cover that somehow defensively, and I tried to do my job, tried not to foul and stay solid, build walls and grab rebounds. And it worked out."

So many in the media had referred to Loyola as a "Cinderella" team during its run to the Final Four. But even the Michigan players took exception to that characterization.

"We don't get into those headlines at this team," said Michigan's Charles Matthews. "We just come out here and play basketball. We never looked at the team as a Cinderella team. It's like 300-something Division I teams, and they're one of the last four standing. That's no Cinderella story. We respected them and we knew we had to come out and execute against them."

Michigan outscored Loyola 47–28 in the second half.

"We…started getting guys going, and Duncan (Robinson) was able to hit shots and Moe was able to hit shots," Michigan freshman Jordan Poole said. "And we're a team that feeds off momentum, so when we were able to get the momentum going in our direction, everything started to go in the right way."

Even Poole got caught up in the aura of Sister Jean and her impact on the Loyola players. Immediately after the game, Poole ran over to her.

"I told her I was a big fan," Poole said. "She got those guys—she had their back the entire time and everybody talks about them being the Cinderella story, and she was getting a lot of attention. But being able to build a fan base how she did, and being able to have Loyola have so many fans out here and travel well…and I just thought the entire concept and every-thing that she brought to the table, and being able to have such a big impact on the team, being in a situation like this, I thought it was amazing.

"Like, the kids don't really get to live in opportunities like this, so having those guys being able to do it and her being behind their back, I thought that was pretty cool."

Beilein had nothing but praise for the Ramblers, not for only their performance in that game, but their entire run to the Final Four.

"I don't know if they had magic on their side. They're good. They wouldn't be here if they were not good. And they beat a Kansas State team that just beat Kentucky. Miami is a very good team," he said.

"They're good. In the NCAA Tournament, everybody is on a neutral floor, and it's so even. And they don't get the opportunity to play home games against schools like Michigan. And they probably never will. And so, as a result, they're good, but people don't know how good they are until you see them out there.

"So they stopped being a Cinderella when they got to the 16, to me, as an 11 seed. The NCAA committee has such a difficult time doing this and everybody can't be a 1 through 4, but there's so little difference between the 4 seed and the 13 seed. It's much smaller a difference than you would think ..."

Beilein talked about the difficulty mid-major schools such as Loyola have when it comes to scheduling big schools like Michigan during the regular season. The big schools lose a great deal of money when playing in a small gym, such as Gentile Arena.

But Beilein conceded, "If Sister Jean asks me, I might even have a better chance of it happening."

Michigan would go on to lose to defending champion Villanova in the championship game in a contest that seemed almost anticlimactic to many college basketball fans caught up in the euphoria Loyola had created.

Indeed the history, tradition and overall mission of Loyola University basketball will continue to evolve through new players, coaches, administrators and fans.

The 2018–19 Ramblers hoped to pick up where the team left off and they started the season with a dominating 76–45 victory over the University of Missouri at Kansas City.

A sell-out crowd at Gentile Arena greeted Loyola players, who took part in a pregame celebration of raising the Final Four banner with roaring approval.

"It was great to see the excitement with the crowd. Obviously you are hoping that this thing can become a great atmosphere to where it becomes a very hard place to play," Moser said after the game. "And I think today was a start. I am greedy. I want sell-outs every game. But I thought the students were really noisy. It was everything you want in a student section. I mean, they were standing, they were loud. Even in the second half. It was fun to see the atmosphere."

Moser continues to emphasize the importance of sustaining a winning style of play, whether it is in a regular-season non-conference contest, a Missouri Valley rivalry game or a postseason tournament matchup.

"I was pleased that we played the right way still," he said after the season-opener. "I thought we were moving it, passing it. Sometimes you start the year and you get a little tight and you try to do things you can't do and not play the way we play. And I thought we were playing and guarding the way we play. That was good to see that right out of the gate."

After several years of watching his teams play in front of a half-empty home arena, Moser sees a future of much greater support from students and other Loyola fans.

"It has just been a long journey to get the atmosphere the way you want it," Moser said. "Someone just showed me a video from two hours before the (UMKC) game. The line (of students) is awesome. It goes on and on and on and on for students. And that's what you want. You want tickets to be a problem here. I just wanted to soak it in. It has been a long journey trying to get this. Think about it. We last year finished last in attendance (in the MVC). It was great to see us pick up with the crowd. It makes a difference. I just took a minute to soak it in and look around. This is what you want in major college basketball."

As much as Moser relished the euphoria of taking his team to the Final Four, his message this season has been to look ahead and strive for new goals. For that reason, he was initially reluctant to take part in the ceremonial lifting of the Final Four banner at Gentile Arena for the season-opener.

"I had mixed emotions to be honest with you," Moser said. "I was a little reluctant because I was so focused on moving forward. There was a moment when I wasn't going to go out, just to be super transparent. Because I was so locked in about moving on and going to the next step. I remember talking to my wife. I just felt that the fans...the banners are nice for fans and all that. And I am glad I did. To be honest with you, I am glad I did. Because it was great to see how excited everyone was. You could look around at people's faces and they were just putting themselves right back in that tournament. So it was a neat moment for the program. That banner will be there forever. So that was great.

"The coach in me was, like, I wanted it to be symbolic that we are moving on. But we went back into the locker room for a minute and we all talked about getting right back to our laser-like focus. And I thought the guys did."

So many new names and faces were considered critical to the Ramblers' hopes in the 2018–19 season. Sharp-shooting freshman Cooper Kaifes was counted on to come off the bench and provide instant offense. Christian Negron, Franklin Agunanne and Isaiah Bujdoso joined Cameron Krutwig, Lucas Williamson, Clayton Custer, Aher Uguak, Marques Townes, Jake Baughman, Bruno Skokna, Will Alcock and Dylan Boehm in hopes of successfully defending the Ramblers' conference title.

"We are going to need to be deep. We are going to need some scoring punch off the bench," Moser said.

"The thing you want to talk about is who we are and we have the shared vision of what you are. And I think the guys believe that together we can be higher than we are individually. When you are together defensively and you are together offensively, you can go a lot higher than you can individually. That is at the core of our culture."

And Loyola basketball history has shown time and time again that teamwork and unselfish play can pay dividends both on and off the court.

Special Acknowledgments

Bill Behrns, Loyola Assistant Athletic Director
The Loyola Athletic Department
Chicago Tribune
Karen Callaway, Photo Editor, ChicagoCatholic.com
Dr. Tom Hitcho, Loyola Senior Associate Athletic Director
ASAP Transcription Services